CONSTRUCTION IN ZAMBIA

JOSEPH CHIRWA
CROSS SILWAMBA

GIFT *Certificate*

TO:

_____

_____

FROM:

_____

_____

DATE: _____

Would you like to buy a copy of
CONSTRUCTION LAW IN ZAMBIA?

PLEASE VISIT:
http://www.diamondbooks.ca

CONSTRUCTION LAW IN ZAMBIA

Joseph Chirwa

He is an academic and law researcher based in the City and Province of Lusaka in the Republic of Zambia.

Cross Silwamba

He is a member of the Engineering Institution of Zambia and is an experienced engineer in both mining and construction.

DIAMOND BOOKS

TM

www.diamondbooks.ca

TORONTO, CANADA – 2022

UNITED STATES, CANADA, SOUTH AFRICA, ZAMBIA, INDIA

CONSTRUCTION LAW IN ZAMBIA

DIAMOND™ BOOKS

www.diamondbooks.ca

PUBLISHED IN CANADA

Published in Canada by DIAMOND BOOKS ™, an imprint
of
DIAMOND PUBLISHERS CANADA
http://www.diamondpublishers.com

DIAMOND BOOKS ™ - REGISTERED TRADEMARK IN CANADA AND WORLDWIDE.

FIRST EDITION: JANUARY, 2022

PAPERBACK EDITION : ISBN: 978-1-77375-203-7

PRINTED IN CANADA

DEDICATION

Joseph Chirwa

To my mother Florence Seyala Mulenshi. I dream of the day I could go back to when I was born. Laying in your arms, wishing you were here today mom. Wish you would appear just for a second from heaven my tears would be gone. One more dance with you mama. Rest in eternal peace ma.

Cross Silwamba

I dedicate this book to God Almighty, my source of inspiration, wisdom, knowledge and understanding.

I also dedicate this work to my family; my wife Angela Byemba Chaila and Children who have encouraged me all the way and whose encouragement has made sure that I give it all it takes to finish that which I have started. My love for you all can never be quantified.

God bless you.

ABOUT THE AUTHORS

Joseph Chirwa

Joseph Chirwa is an academic and law researcher based in the City and Province of Lusaka in the Republic of Zambia. He has taught law in various subjects at all leading law schools in the country which include that of the University of Zambia, University of Lusaka, Mulungushi University, Zambian Open University, Zambia Centre for Accountancy Studies University and the National Institute of Public Administration among others.

Mr Chirwa was admitted as an Advocate of the High Court for Zambia on 19th April, 2018 and is an Advocate with audience in all the Superior Courts of Zambia. He is a qualified legal draftsperson and an author of many leading law texts on various areas of the law in Zambia. He has practiced law at the Attorney-General's Chambers, Anti-Corruption Commission and Zambia Telecommunications Company Limited. He is currently working in private practice under the name and style of Messrs Ferd Jere and Company.

Mr Chirwa is the Executive Director of the not-for-profit Institute of Law, Policy Research and Human Rights, a think tank on good governance and rule of law, constitutionalism, policy and human rights which he founded in 2020.

Cross Silwamba

Cross Silwamba is a member of the Engineering Institution of Zambia and is an experienced engineer in both mining and construction. He is part of management at Konkola Copper Mine a company he joined in 2005.

He is a graduate and alumni of the University of Zambia and Copperbelt University where he studied Bachelor of Science in Mining Engineering and Master of Science in Rock Slope Engineering. He is currently studying Bachelor of Laws Degree at the University of Zambia.

ACKNOWLEDGEMENTS

We wish to give praise and thanks to the Lord God Almighty for blessing us with the gift of life and writing. According to the Gospel of John, the Lord God decreed that "I will not leave you as orphans, I will come to you!" Lord God you have seen us through from nothing and may your word be glorified and praised forever.

PREFACE

This book is an attempt to bring to the fore salient issues surrounding the construction industry as it relates to architects, engineers, contractors, planners and surveyors among other allied professionals. This has been done in such a manner that case law and legislation have been dissected and explained for the assimilation of both non-lawyers and lawyers alike in what would be called a "crash course". The book has covered salient topics of interest to these professions such as the following:

- Legal environment of construction law
- Institutional framework of construction law
- Professional conduct and ethics
- Alternative dispute resolution
- Employment and labour relations
- Occupational health and safety
- Business associations
- Contract, criminal and tortious liability
- Commercial transactions
- Intellectual property
- Insurance
- Property relations
- Securities law

- Environmental law and policy
- Competition and consumer protection

JC and CS, Lusaka, 2022.

TABLE OF CONTENTS

TABLE OF STATUTES

Employment Code Act No. 3 of 2019

Engineering Institution of Zambia Act No. 17 of 2010

English Law (Extent of Application) Act, Chapter 11 of the Laws of Zambia

Environmental Management Act No. 12 of 2011

Forests Act No. 4 of 2015

Gazette Notice No. 1345 of 1975

Gender Equity and Equality Act No. 22 of 2015

Government Gazette No. 836 of 2016

High Court (Amendment) Rules of 1997 (S.I. No. 71 of 1997)

High Court (Amendment) Rules, 2020 (S.I. No. 58 of 2020)

ILO Convention No. 87 of 1948

ILO Convention No. 98 of 1949

Income Tax, Chapter 323 of the Laws of Zambia

Industrial and Labor Relations Act, Chapter 269 of the Laws of Zambia

Insurance Act No. 11 of 1997

Interpretation and General Provisions Act, Chapter 2 of the Laws of Zambia

Land Survey Act, Chapter 188 of the Laws of Zambia

Lands Acquisition Act, Chapter 189 of the Laws of Zambia

Lands Act, Chapter 184 of the Laws of Zambia

Lands and Deeds Registry Act, Chapter 185 of the Laws of Zambia

Lands Tribunal Act No. 39 of 2010

Local Authorities Superannuation Fund Act, Chapter 284 of the Laws of Zambia

Mental Health Act No. 6 of 2019

Mines and Minerals Development Act No. 11 of 2015

National Council for Construction Act No. 13 of 2003

National Health Insurance Act No. 2 of 2018

National Pension Scheme Authority Act, Chapter 256 of the Laws of Zambia

Occupational Health and Safety Act No. 36 of 2010

Occupier's Liability Act, Chapter 70 of the Laws of Zambia

Partnership Act, 1890

Patents Act No. 40 of 2016

Pension Scheme Regulation (Amendment) Act No. 27 of 2005

Pension Scheme Regulation Act No. 28 of 1996

Pension Scheme Regulation Act, Chapter 255 of the Laws of Zambia

Persons with Disabilities Act No. 6 of 2012

Public Health Act (Building Regulations) Act, Chapter 295 of the Laws of Zambia

Public Private Partnerships Act No. 14 of 2009

Public Procurement Act No. 12 of 2008

Public Roads Act No. 12 of 2002

Public Service Pensions Act No. 35 of 1996

Quantity Surveyors Act, Chapter 438 of the Laws of Zambia

Ratings Act No. 12 of 1997

Registered Designs Act, Chapter 402 of the Laws of Zambia

Registration of Business Names Act No. 16 of 2011

Rules of the Supreme Court of England, 1999 Edition

Sale of Goods Act, 1893

Sheriffs Act, Chapter 37 of the Laws of Zambia

Statutory Functions Act, Chapter 4 of the Laws of Zambia

Statutory Instrument No. 7 of 1964

Statutory Instrument No. 89 of 1996

Town and Country Planning, Chapter 283 of the Laws of Zambia

Trade Marks Act, Chapter 401 of the Laws of Zambia

Urban and Regional Planners Act No. 4 of 2011

Urban and Regional Planning Act No. 3 of 2015

Valuation Surveyors Act, Chapter 207 of the Laws of Zambia

Water Resources Management Act No. 21 of 2011

Workers' Compensation Act No. 10 of 1999

Zambia Institute of Architects Act, Chapter 442 of the Laws of Zambia

Zambia Wildlife Act No. 14 of 2015

LIST OF CASES

African Banking Corp v Goldman Insurance Ltd 2007/HPC/0212

Alder v Dickinson [1954] 3 All ER 396

AMF International Ltd v Magnet Bowling Ltd [1968] 2 All ER 789

Amiran v Agriflora (Z) Ltd (In Receivership) 2004/HP/0268

Anglo-African Shipping Co of New York Inc. v J Mortner Ltd [1962] 1 Lloyd's Rep 610

Armstrong v Jackson (1917) 2 KBD 822 at 826

Associated Chemicals Ltd v Hill & Delamain and Ellis & Co (1998) ZR 9

Associated Chemicals Ltd v Hill & Delamain Zambia Ltd and Ellis & Co. (As a Law Firm), SCZ Judgement No. 2 of 1998

Attorney-General and Another v Ireen Mohingi Lemba (2008) ZR 215

Attorney-General and the Labor Commissioner v Zulu, Kamukwamba, Mundia, Muyangwa and Others [1995-1997] ZR 33 (SC)

Attorney-General of Duchy of Lancaster v Overton Ltd [1982] 1 All ER 524

Attorney-General v E.B. Jones Machinists Ltd (2000) ZR 114

Clement H. Mweempe v Attorney-General and Interpol (2012) 2 ZR 155

Coles v Enoch (1939)3 All ER 327

Collett v Van Zyl Bros. Ltd (1966) ZR 65 (CA)

Credit Africa Bank Ltd (In Liquidation) v John Dingani Mudenda (2003) ZR 66

Curie v Misa 1875) LR 10 Exch 153

Datec Electronic Holdings Ltd v United Parcels Service Ltd [2007] UKHL 23

Development Bnak of Zambia v JCN Holdings Ltd and Others (Appeal No. 54/2016)

DPP v Gomez (1993) AC 442

Drake and Gorham (Z) Ltd v Energo Project Ltd (1990) ZR 58

Dunlop Tyre v Selfridge [1915] AC 847

Eastern Distributors Ltd v Goldring (1957) 2 QB 600

Edith Solomon v Duncan Gilbey and Matheson (Z) Ltd, Complaint No. 17 of 1985

Edwards v Skyways [1964] 1 All ER 494

Entick v Carrington (1765) 2 Wils. KB 275

Esso Petroleum Ltd v Customs and Excise Commissioners [1976] 1 WLR 1

Fagan v Metropolitan Police Commissioner [1961] 1 QBD 439

G (A) v G (T) (1970) 2 QB 643

Garmon Ltd v Attorney-General of Hong Kong [1985] 1 AC 1 (Privy Council)

General Cleaning Contractors v Christmas [1953] A.C. 180

George Lewis v Zimco Limited (1992) S.J. (S.C)

Goodwin v Reilley, 1 Dist., 176 Cal. App. 3d 86, 221, Cal.Rptr. 374, 376

Government Stock and Securities Investments Co. v Manila Railway Co. [1897] AC 81

Grayson Kachikoti v Tap Building Products Ltd, Complaint No. 33 of 1982

Gregory v Piper [1829] 9 B & C 591

Harvey v Johnson (1848) 6 CB 295

Hinde v Whitehouse (1806) 7 East 558

Howell v Coupland (1876) 1 QBD 258

Hudson v Ridge Manufacturing [1957] 2 Q.B. 348

Hunter v Canary Wharf [1997] AC 655

Hurst v Picture Theatres Ltd [1915] 1 KB 1

Illingworth v Houldsworth (1904) AC 355

Intermarket Banking Corp. v Goldman Insurance Co., Appeal No.125 of 2017

Ireland v Livingston (1872) LR 5 HL 395

Itowala v Variety Bureau de Change (2001) ZR 96

John Young and Co. v The Bankier Distillery Co. [1893] AC 691

Jones v Padavatton [1969] 2 All ER 616

Judith Namposya v Hoechst (Z) Ltd, Complaint No. 62 of 1985

Kalusha Bwalya v Chadore Properties Ltd and Another, 2009/HPC/0294

Kariba North Bank Ltd v PFM Shewell (1985) ZR 150 (SC)

Kasabi Industries Ltd v Intermarket Banking Corp. Ltd Appeal No. 168 of 2009

Keembe Estates Ltd v Galaunia Farms Ltd, SCZ Appeal No. 33 of 2003

Keith Spicer, Ltd v Mansell [1970] 1 All ER 462

Kleinwort Benson v Malaysia Mining Corporation [1989] 1 All ER 785

Koufour v Greenberg (1982) ZR 30 (HC)

Lawrence v Obee (1814) 3 Camp 514

Lee v Bayes (1856) 18 CB 601

Lee v Lee's Air Farming Ltd (1961) AC 12

Lloyd Mwiya Milupi v Zambia Seed Company Limited, Complaint No. 19 of 1982

Lonrho Cotton (Z) Ltd v Mukuba Textiles Ltd (2000) ZR 43

[1994] 4 All ER 286 (QBDC)

Naval Colliery Co. Ltd v Inland Revenue Commissioners (1928) 138 LT 593

Norman v Overseas Motor Transport (Tanganyika) Ltd (1959) EALR 131 (CAEA)

Nyimba Investments Ltd v Nico Insurance Zambia Ltd, Selected Judgement No. 12 of 2017

Oscar Chess Ltd v Williams (1957) 1 WLR 370

Paddington Churches Association v Technical and General Guarantee Co. Ltd 1999 BLR 244

Parker v Clarke [1960] 1 All ER 93

Parry v Cleaver [1970] AC 1

Patel's Bazaar Ltd v The People (1965) ZR 84 (CA)

 Pharmaceutical Society of Great Britain v Storkwain Ltd (1986) 83 Cr. App. R. 359 (HL)

Pigott B. in Bradburn v The Great Western Railway Co. (1874) LR 10 Exch 1

Pillans v Van Mierop (1765) 3 Burr. 1663

Power Equipment Ltd v Goldtronics Ltd and Barclays Bank PLC (1998/HP/1946)

R v Gateway Foodmarkets Ltd [1997] 2 Cr. App. R. 40

R v Registrar of Companies (1931) 2 KB 197

R v Registrar of Companies Ex parte Bowen [1914] 3 KB 1161

Scruttons v Midlands Silicones [1962] AC 446 (HL)

Settlement Trustees v Nuran (1970) EALR 570

Shanklin Pier v Detel Products [1951] 2KB 854

Short v Treasury Commissioners (1948) 1 KB 122

Simpkins v Pays [1955] 3 All ER 10

Simpson v Weber (1925) 41 TLR 302

Smith v Stone (1647) 82 ER 533

Sobell Industries Ltd v Cory Bros & Co [1955] 2 Lloyd's Rep 82

Stekel v Ellice [1973] 1 All ER 465

Stevens v Biller (1883) 25 Ch. D 31

Stocks v Wilson (1913) 2 KB 235; and Imperial Loan Co v Stone (1892) 1 QB 599

Storer v Manchester CC [1974] 1 WLR 1403

Tata Engineering and Locomotive Co. Ltd v State of Bihar 1965 AIR 40

Taylor v Robinson (1818) 2 Moore CP 730; and Dixon v Stansfeld (1850) 10 CB 398

Taylor v Rover [1966] 1 W.L.R. 1491

Tennent v Tennent (1870) LR 2 Sc. & Div. 6

Tesco Supermarkets Ltd v Mattrass 1972] AC 153 (HL)

Thabo Meli v R [1954] 1 All ER 373 (Privy Council)

Georgoupollos (1972) ZR 288 (HC)

Zambia Consolidated Copper Mines Plc. and Ndola Lime Ltd v Sikanyika and Others, SCZ Judgement No. 24 of 202

Zambia National Provident Fund Board v Rowlands Musukwa, SCZ Judgement No. 15 of 1995

Zambia State Insurance Corp v Sasol Fertilizers (Z) Ltd Appeal No. 158 of 2001

CHAPTER

1

❧

LEGAL ENVIRONMENT OF
CONSTRUCTION LAW

1.0 Introduction

This Chapter examines the legal environment as it relates to construction law in Zambia. The Chapter will look at the laws that relate to architects, engineers and contractors in this jurisdiction. It will also trace the constitutional basis of construction law to specific statutes that have an impact on this field of law.

1.1 Constitution of Zambia

What is a Constitution?

A constitution is a body of rules, conventions and practices which describe, regulate or qualify the organization, powers and operation of government and the relations between persons and public authorities.[1] It is the organic and fundamental law of a nation or state, which may be written

---

[1] Turpin, C. and Tomkins, A. (2007). British Government and the Constitution, 6th edn., Cambridge: Cambridge University Press at p.4

or unwritten, establishing the character and conception of its government, laying the basic principles to which its internal life is to be conformed, organizing the government, and regulating, distributing, and limiting the functions of its different departments, and prescribing the extent and manner of the exercise of sovereign powers.[2]

The nature of the Zambian Constitution

The Constitution of Zambia is a written document that espouses the above characteristics. It is a document adopted by the people for the people to govern themselves. The people are the source of all sovereign authority and power, and it is the people who adopt and give to themselves the Constitution for their own self-governance.[3] It must be noted that the legislative, executive and judicial authority derives from the people of Zambia who vests that authority in the respective organs of government.[4]

Principles relating to land, environment, and natural resources

Construction law is closely related to the management of land, environment and natural resources. This is so because the exploitation of land, environment and natural resources are closely interlinked with the overall framework of the work of engineers, architects and contractors. It is thus

---

[2] Black, H.C. et al (1990). Black's Law Dictionary, 6th edn., Minnesota: West Publishing Co. at p.311
[3] Preamble to the Constitution of Zambia, Chapter 1 of the Laws of Zambia as amended by Act No. 2 of 2016
[4] See Articles 61, 90 and 118 (1) of the Constitution of Zambia (Amendment) Act No. 2 of 2016

imperative that these professionals know the underlying principles of land, environment and natural resource use in this country as this is undeniably the foundation upon which Construction law is premised.

i. Principles of land policy

The Principles of land policy in Zambia are found under Article 253 of the Constitution of Zambia. The engineer, architect and contractor as well as the construction lawyer must be conversant with the principles that govern land alienation and use in this country. The ultimate thesis of these principles is that land must only be used in a manner that promotes sustainable development and follows the law relating to its alienation and use. The above-said provisions state as follows:

(1) Land shall be held, used and managed in accordance with the following principles:

(a) Equitable access to land and associated resources;

(b) Security of tenure for lawful land holders;

(c) Recognition of indigenous cultural rites;

(d) Sustainable use of land;

(e) Transparent, effective and efficient administration of land;

(f) Effective and efficient settlement of land disputes;

(g) River frontages, islands, lakeshores and ecologically and culturally sensitive areas—

(i) To be accessible to the public;

(ii) Not to be leased, fenced or sold; and

(iii) To be maintained and used for conservation and preservation activities;

(h) Investments in land to also benefit local communities and their economy; and

(i) Plans for land use to be done in a consultative and participatory manner.

ii. Principles of environmental and natural resources management and development

The knowledge of the principles of land policy in this jurisdiction is useless if it is not accompanied with the knowledge of the policy that govern the environment and use of natural resources. As stated above, the work of engineers, architects and contractors touch on the environment and exploitation of natural resources. It becomes a no-brainer that an engineer, architect or contractor must know the principles surrounding these two before they can efficiently and effectively advise clients and embark on projects. The principles regarding the environment and natural resources management and development are found under Articles 255, 256 and 257 of the Constitution which provide as follows:

255. The management and development of Zambia's environment and natural resources shall be governed by the following principles:

(a) Natural resources have an environmental, economic, social and cultural value and this shall be reflected in their use;

(b) The person responsible for polluting or degrading the environment is responsible for paying for the damage done to the environment;

(c) Where there are threats of serious or irreversible damage to the environment, lack of full scientific certainty shall not be used as a reason for postponing cost-effective measures to prevent environmental degradation;

(d) The conservation and protection of ecologically sensitive areas, habitats, and species shall be done in a sustainable manner;

(e) Respect for the integrity of natural processes and ecological communities;

(f) Benefits accruing from the exploitation and utilization of the environment and natural resources shall be shared equitably amongst the people of Zambia;

(g) Saving of energy and the sustainable use of renewable energy sources shall be promoted;

(h) Reclaiming and rehabilitation of degraded areas and those prone to disasters shall be promoted;

(i) Equitable access to environmental resources shall be promoted;

(j) Effective participation of people in the development of relevant policies, plans and programmes; and

(k) Access to environmental information to enable people preserve, protect and conserve the environment.

256. A person has a duty to co-operate with State organs, State institutions and other persons to—

(a) Maintain a clean, safe and healthy environment;

(b) Ensure ecologically sustainable development and use of natural resources;

(c) Respect, protect and safeguard the environment; and

(d) Prevent or discontinue an act which is harmful to the environment.

257. The State shall, in the utilisation of natural resources and management of the environment—

(a) Protect genetic resources and biological diversity;

(b) Implement mechanisms that minimise waste;

(c) Promote appropriate environmental management systems and tools;

(d) Encourage public participation;

(e) Protect and enhance the intellectual property in, and indigenous knowledge of, biodiversity and genetic resources of local communities;

(f) Ensure that the environmental standards enforced in Zambia are of essential benefit to citizens; and

(g) Establish and implement mechanisms that address climate change.

1.2 Legislation

The legislation that governs the construction industry may be categorized into what can be called regulatory laws and operational (or enabling) laws. The regulatory laws deal with the registration, licensing and qualification of professions involved in the construction industry while the operational laws are concerned with laying the platform for the smooth running of the construction business.

i. Regulatory Laws

National Council for Construction Act

The National Council for Construction Act No. 13 of 2003 (hereinafter referred to as the "NCC" Act) is the main piece of legislation that governs the construction industry in Zambia. The objectives of this Act as enunciated in its Preamble are to among others provide for the:

(a) Establishment of the National Council for Construction and to define its functions;

(b) Promotion and development of the construction industry in Zambia; to provide for the registration of contractors;

(c) Affiliation to the Council of professional bodies or organizations whose members are engaged in activities related to the construction industry;

(d) Regulation of the construction industry; to provide for the establishment of the Construction School; and

(e) Training of persons engaged in construction or in activities related to construction.

The functions of the National Construction Council are espoused under section 5 of the Act which are to:

(a) Promote and develop the construction industry in Zambia, and give priority to Zambian Companies;

(b) Assess the performance of contractors in the execution of contracts and thus provide a performance record for contractors;

(c) Regulate the behaviour and promote minimum standards and best practice of contractors;

(d) Provide data on the size and distribution of contractors operating within the industry;

(e) Facilitate, where possible, access by Zambian Companies to resources for the development of their operations;

(f) Promote, in liaison with other bodies in construction related fields, development issues relating to the construction industry;

(g) Promote research into construction and the development and use of local materials and appropriate construction materials;

(h) In consultation with the National Housing Authority, the Director in the Buildings Department and other bodies, promote the construction of low cost and medium density housing;

(i) Set and promote safety standards in the construction industry;

(j) Prescribe and vary the categories for the registration of persons engaged in the construction industry;

(k) Conduct training and co-ordinate the training programmes of persons engaged in the construction industry;

(l) Make available to persons engaged in the construction industry, published information, advice and assistance in relation to the construction industry;

(m) Monitor and evaluate, from time to time, the capacity and progress of persons engaged in the construction industry;

(n) Promote and maintain competition among the professionals or other persons engaged in the construction industry and promote efficiency and economy on the part of the professionals and persons so engaged;

(o) Regulate activities in the construction industry through the appropriate institutions, Boards and other authorities, as the case may be;

(p) Co-ordinate construction related activities;

(q) Formulate policies and programmes of the School;

(r) Recommend to the Minister the conditions under which a foreign company may be registered and permitted to operate in Zambia;

(s) Review, from time to time, the process of awarding contracts; and

(t) Standardise quality control, contract documentation, codes of practice, procurement processes, legal and contractual processes in liaison with other relevant bodies or organizations and in accordance with other written laws.

The Council also has the mandate to register and deregister contractors in this jurisdiction.[5] It is also law that professional bodies that regulate architects, engineers and surveyors must be affiliated to the NCC.[6] It is also within the Council's mandate to register projects to gather information on the nature, value and distribution of projects and provide the basis for a best practice project assessment scheme provided for under NCC Act.[7] The Construction School established under section 17 of the Act is also subjected to the control of the Council as stipulated under section 20 of the same Act. The Council has the authority to appoint a Principal and staff of the Construction School[8] and its powers in relation to the School are as follows:

(a) Set minimum educational and, other qualifications or requirements for persons seeking enrolment as students of the School;

(b) Enrol students at the School and keep a register of all such enrolled students;

(c) Determine fees to be paid by any member of an affiliated body or other person in respect of courses, workshops, seminars or examinations set by the Council;

---

[5] Part III of the NCC Act, sections 7 and 10
[6] Section 12
[7] Section 15 (1)
[8] Section 18

(d) Set and establish courses of study or syllabi as it considers necessary;

(e) Confer certificates on persons who are successful candidates in the examinations conducted by the Council or upon participation in workshops or seminars offered at, by, or under the auspices of the School;

(f) Provide high quality training, research and consultancy in construction;

(g) Develop the capacity of the School in teaching, research and consultancy related to construction;

(h) Provide high quality training in research, consultancy and management for persons engaged in construction or related fields;

(i) Improve the quality and standard of construction management as a means of encouraging productivity and efficiency;

(j) Improve the capacity of persons engaged in construction;

(k) Make rules, in consultation with the Principal, for the regulation of the affairs of the students of the School; and

(l) In consultation with the Principal set out guidelines for generating and investing funds for the sustainable operation of the School.

Offences under the NCC Act

Offences and penalties (Section 21)

(1)   A contractor shall not undertake, carry out or complete any construction works or portion of such works for a public sector contract, awarded in terms of competitive tender or quotation, unless the contractor is registered with the Council and holds a valid certificate issued by the Council.

(2)   Any person who contravenes subsection (1) commits an offence and shall be liable, on conviction, to a fine not exceeding one hundred thousand penalty units or to imprisonment for a period not exceeding two years, or to both.

(3)   An employee of a contractor registered under the Act shall not be deemed to carry on business within the meaning of this section by reason only of the performance of that person's functions as an employee.

(4)   Any contractor who carries out or attempts to carry out any construction works or portion of such works under a public sector contract and who is not a registered contractor or after being notified in writing that the certificate of registration has been cancelled commits an offence and shall be liable, on conviction, to a fine not exceeding one hundred thousand penalty

units or to imprisonment for a period not exceeding two years, or to both.

(5) In this section, *"public sector contract"* means a contract in respect of construction works for the Government, a parastatal or a statutory body.

Prohibition in respect of award of tender unless registered (Section 22)

(1) A person shall not award a contract for any construction works of such value as the Minister may, by statutory instrument, upon the recommendation of the Council, determine to another person unless that other person is registered under this Act.

(2) A person who contravenes subsection (1) commits an offence and shall be liable, on conviction, to a fine not exceeding one hundred thousand penalty units or to imprisonment for a period not exceeding two years, or to both.

Award of contract to foreign company (Section 23)

(1) A person shall not award a contract for construction works to a foreign firm without the approval of the Council.

(2) Where an award for a contract is referred to the Council for approval and the Council determines that the construction work to be awarded can be undertaken by a Zambian company the Council shall

not endorse its approval and the person shall not award the contract to the foreign company.

(3) A person who contravenes subsection (1) or (2) commits an offence and shall be liable, on conviction, to a penalty not exceeding one hundred thousand penalty units or to imprisonment for a term not exceeding two years, or to both.

Partnership with Zambian company (Section 24)

(1) Subject to section sixteen a person shall not award a contract for any construction works to a foreign company unless the foreign company undertakes the construction works in partnership or jointly with a Zambian company.

(2) A person who contravenes subsection (1) commits an offence and shall be liable, on conviction, to a fine not exceeding one hundred thousand penalty units or to imprisonment for a term not exceeding two years, or to both.

Prohibition of use of substandard construction materials (Section 25)

(1) A contractor shall not use—

(a) Construction materials; or

(b) Other materials used in the construction industry or construction related activities that do not conform to the standards set under the standards act or that are of a substandard quality.

(2) A person who contravenes subsection (1) commits an offence and shall be liable, on conviction, to a fine not exceeding one hundred thousand penalty units or to imprisonment for a term not exceeding two years, or to both.

Manufacture or sale of substandard construction materials (Section 26)

(1) A person shall not manufacture or sell—

(a) Construction materials; or

(b) Other materials used in the construction industry or construction related activities that do not conform to the standards set under the standards act or that are of a substandard quality.

(2) A person who contravenes subsection (1) commits an offence and shall be liable, on conviction, to a fine not exceeding one hundred thousand penalty units or to imprisonment for a term not exceeding two years, or to both.

Engineering Institution of Zambia Act

The Engineering Institution of Zambia Act No. 17 of 2010 (hereinafter referred to as the "EIZ Act") is the main piece of legislation regulating the engineering profession. The

Act sets professional standards for the practice of the engineering profession and furnishes the code of conduct, categories of membership and a fraternity for engineers and allied professionals. This is an Act, as per its Preamble, to:

> Continue the existence of the Engineering Institution of Zambia; provide for the registration of engineering professionals, engineering units and engineering organisations and regulate their professional conduct; repeal the Engineering Institution of Zambia Act, 1992; and provide for matters connected with, or incidental to, the foregoing.

Section 3 creates the Engineering Institution of Zambia (EIZ) as a body corporate with perpetual succession and a common seal, capable of suing and being sued in its corporate name and shall, subject to the provisions of this Act, have power to do all such acts and things as a body corporate may, by law, do or perform. The functions of the EIZ are as follows as provided under section 4 of the Act:

(a) Register engineering professionals, engineering organisations and engineering units and regulate their professional conduct;

(b) Register students of engineering;

(c) Develop, promote, maintain and improve appropriate standards of qualification in the engineering profession;

(d) Develop, promote and enforce internationally comparable engineering practice standards in Zambia;

(e) Investigate allegations of professional misconduct and impose such sanctions as may be necessary;

(f) Advise the government on matters relating to the engineering profession;

(g) Promote the general advancement of science, engineering, technological and allied disciplines for the improvement of the quality of life;

(h) Maintain and improve the standards of conduct and learning of science, engineering and allied professions in Zambia;

(i) Facilitate the acquisition of knowledge by engineering professionals through the establishment of technical libraries, and the provision of monetary grants, books, apparatus and any other facilities necessary to achieve this end;

(j) Hold meetings of the institution for the reading and discussion of papers for professional interest, to make awards to authors of papers of special merit and to arrange for other activities of interest or benefit to engineering professionals;

(k) Raise the character and status of the engineering profession and allied disciplines, to promote honourable and good practice and increase the confidence of the community in those persons practicing in the engineering profession and allied disciplines;

(l) Promote alternative dispute resolution mechanisms and to serve as an arbitral institution for disputes of an engineering nature;

(m) In consultation with the ministry responsible for education and the technical education vocational and entrepreneurship training authority, accredit universities, technical colleges, institutions and programmes of instruction leading to the award of qualifications of membership classes;

(n) Investigate and monitor national emergencies or disasters or any other matter of public concern caused by, or likely to be caused by, an engineering product or service and recommend appropriate preventive, rehabilitative or other measures; and

(o) Represent, protect and assist engineering professionals regarding their conditions of practice, remuneration or otherwise.

The management and control of the affairs of the EIZ are discharged by the Council which is established under section 8 of the Act while the registration and cancellation of registration is done by the Engineering Registration Board established under section 12 of the

Act. The functions of the Council include the following as outlined under section 9 of the Act:

(a) Perform all the functions of the Institution;

(b) Promote an understanding of professional ethics amongst the engineering professionals;

(c) Ensure that the rules and guidelines for professional ethics developed by the Institution are responsive to the expectations of business institutions, the public and those who rely on engineering work;

(d) Participate in the development of international engineering practice standard setting;

(e) Make recommendations affecting, or relating to the engineering profession to the general meeting of the Institution;

(f) Register students of engineering;

(g) Promote continuing professional development among engineering professionals; and

(h) Do all such things and acts as the Institution or Council may do under this Act.

Offences under the EIZ Act

Prohibition of person practicing without registration (Section 15)

(1) A person shall not practise as an engineering professional, unless that person is registered as a Member, under the constitution of the Institution, and as an engineering professional, in accordance with this Act.

(2) A person who contravenes subsection (1) commits an offence and is liable, upon conviction, to a fine not exceeding one million penalty units or to imprisonment for a period not exceeding ten years, or to both.

Prohibition of engineering organization or engineering unit practicing without registration (Section 18)

(1) An engineering organization or engineering unit shall not provide any engineering service or product, unless that engineering organization or engineering unit is registered in accordance with this Act.

(2) An engineering organization or engineering unit that contravenes subsection (1) commits an offence and is liable, upon conviction, to a fine not exceeding nine hundred thousand penalty units.

Prohibition of practice without practicing certificate (Section 25)

(1) A person shall not practise as an engineering professional, unless that person holds a practicing certificate issued by the Board under this Act.

(2) A person who contravenes subsection (1) commits an offence and is liable, upon conviction, to a fine not exceeding seven hundred thousand penalty units or to imprisonment for a period not exceeding seven years, or to both.

Cancellation of practicing certificate (Section 30)

(1) The Board shall cancel a practicing certificate if the holder—

(a) Is found guilty of any professional misconduct;

(b) Is declared to be of unsound mind;

(c) Is bankrupt;

(d) Contravenes the provisions of any law;

(e) Obtained the practicing certificate through fraud, misrepresentation or concealment of a material fact; or

(f) Commits an offence under this act or contravenes the code of ethics.

(2)   Where a certificate of registration is cancelled under this Act, the practicing certificate held by the holder of the certificate of registration shall be void and shall be surrendered to the Board.

(3)   The Board shall, before cancelling a practicing certificate under this section, give the holder of the practicing certificate an opportunity to be heard.

(4)   The Board may, before cancelling the practicing certificate of an engineering professional, suspend the holder of the practicing certificate for such period and on such terms and conditions as the Board may determine.

Holding out as an engineering professional, engineering organisation, etc. (Section 41)

(1)   A person shall not, unless the person is registered as an engineering professional, engineering organisation or engineering unit under this Act—

(a) Practise as, be employed as, offer engineering services, be engaged as an agent of, or hold out to be, an engineering professional, engineering organisation or engineering unit;

(b) Adopt, use or exhibit the titles *"registered engineering organisation," "registered engineering unit", "registered engineer", "registered technologist", "registered technician," "registered craftsperson"* or any other title or abbreviation of like description; or

(c) Do anything likely to lead persons to infer that the person is a registered engineering professional, engineering organisation or engineering unit.

(2) A person or body corporate shall not offer employment to a person requiring registration under this Act.

(3) A person who contravenes subsection (1) or (2) commits an offence and is liable, upon conviction, to a fine not exceeding one million penalty units or to imprisonment for a period not exceeding ten years, or to both.

(4) An engineering professional, engineering organisation or engineering unit shall not permit the engineering professional's, engineering organization's or engineering unit's name to be used by a person who is not a registered engineering professional, engineering organisation or engineering unit.

(5) A person who contravenes subsection (4) commits an offence and is liable, upon conviction, to a fine not exceeding one million penalty units or to imprisonment for a period not exceeding ten years, or to both.

(6) Where an engineering organisation or engineering unit commits an act which if done by an individual would be an offence under subsection (3), every partner in that organisation or unit shall be deemed to have

committed the offence unless the partner proves that the offence was committed without the other partner(s)' knowledge or consent.

Offences regarding registered engineering professional, engineering organisation, etc. (Section 43)

(1) A person shall not —

(a) Make or cause to be made an unauthorised entry, alteration or erasure in the Register or a certified copy of an entry in the Register or a certificate of registration or other certificate issued under this Act;

(b) Impersonate or use the title of a registered engineering professional, engineering organisation or engineering unit while not registered as such under this Act;

(c) Procure, or attempt to procure, registration under this Act, by fraud, misrepresentation or the concealment of a material fact; or

(d) Forge a certificate of registration or other certificate issued under this Act.

(2) A person who contravenes subsection (1), commits an offence and is liable, upon conviction, to a fine not exceeding one million penalty units or to imprisonment for a period not exceeding ten years, or to both.

Professional misconduct (Section 46)

An engineering professional, engineering organisation or engineering unit commits professional misconduct if the engineering professional, engineering organisation or engineering unit—

(a) Contravenes the provisions of this Act;

(b) Unlawfully discloses or uses to the advantage of the engineering professional, engineering organisation or engineering unit any information acquired in the practice of the engineering profession, engineering organisation or engineering unit;

(c) Engages in conduct that is dishonest, fraudulent or deceitful;

(d) Commits an offence under any other law;

(e) Engages in any conduct that is prejudicial to the engineering profession or is likely to bring it into disrepute; or

(f) Breaches the Code of Ethics or encourages another engineering professional, engineering organisation or engineering unit to breach or disregard the principles of the Code of Ethics.

(g) General penalty (Section 59)

A person who contravenes a provision of this Act for which a specific penalty is not provided, is liable, upon conviction, to a fine not exceeding one hundred thousand penalty units or to imprisonment for a period not exceeding one year, or to both.

Offences by body corporate or unincorporated body (Section 60)

Where an offence under this Act is committed by a body corporate or an unincorporated body, every director or manager of the body corporate or an unincorporated body shall be liable, upon conviction, as if the director or manager had personally committed the offence, unless the director or manager proves to the satisfaction of the court that the act constituting the offence was done without the knowledge, consent or connivance of the director or manager or that the director or manager took reasonable steps to prevent the commission of the offence.

Zambia Institute of Architects Act

The Zambia Institute of Architects (ZIA) is one of the oldest professional groupings in the Republic. ZIA is a regulatory body created by the Zambia Institute of Architects Act, Chapter 442 of the Laws of Zambia (hereinafter referred to as the "ZIA Act").[9] The management and control of the affairs of ZIA are discharged by the Council as established by section 14 of

---

[9] Section 3

the Act. Some of the functions of the Institute are the following:

(a) Promote the general advancement of architecture and facilitate the acquiring of knowledge in architecture and the allied professions;

(b) Provide for the registration of architects;

(c) Promote good architectural practice;

(d) Maintain and improve the standards and conduct of architects;

(e) Consider allegations of professional misconduct of architects; and

(f) All other things incidental, or conducive, to the attainment of the functions of the institute.

The Council of the Institute is mandated to exercise the functions of the Institute; to issue membership certificates to approve applicants; and to ratify decisions of the Disciplinary Committee.[10] This is opposed to the registration of architects which function is reposed in the Honorary Secretary as espoused by section 28 of the Act upon one meeting the qualifications as set out under section 29 of the same Act.

---

[10] Section 15

Offences under the ZIA Act

Professional misconduct (Section 25)

A registered architect shall be guilty of professional misconduct if, during his practice, he –

(a) Allows any person, other than a registered architect or trainee architect in his employment to practise in the name of a registered architect;

(b) Unlawfully discloses or uses to his own advantage, any information which was acquired in the course of his professional work on behalf of his client;

(c) Certifies or submits in his name or in the names of his firm a report, document, drawing, statement and related records which have not been made by him, his partner or an architect employed by his company;

(d) Permits his name or the name of his company to be used in connection with technical specifications, designs or financial calculations which are not accurate;

(e) Charges for professional work and fees other than the scales approved by the council;

(f) Fails to disclose or knowingly conceals from his client information or facts, which may mislead his client; or

(g) Gives incorrect or insufficient professional advice.

Penalties to be imposed by Disciplinary Committee (Section 26)

(1) Where the Disciplinary Committee, after due inquiry finds an architect guilty of professional misconduct, it may impose one or more of the following penalties:

(a) Order the cancellation of his practising certificate;

(b) Recommend to the council, the –

(i) Suspension of any member and impose any reasonable conditions for the postponement or suspension for a period not exceeding two years;

(ii) Expulsion; or

(c) Censure him.

(2) The Disciplinary Committee shall as soon as practicable after the completion of each hearing, submit a report of the proceedings, together with a copy of the record kept to the Council.

Disqualification of architects (Section 30)

A person shall not qualify to be registered as an architect if –

(a) He has been convicted of an offence involving dishonesty;

(b) He has been adjudged or otherwise declared to be of unsound mind under any law in force in Zambia;

(c) He is an undischarged bankrupt; or

(d) In the case of a company, the company is not registered with the institute.

Offences relating to practising certificate (Section 35)

(1) A person not registered by the Council, shall not -

(a) Establish a practice as an architect or be a partner in any architectural firm;

(b) Practise or offer his services as, or hold himself out to be, a qualified architect, consultant or advisor;

(c) Adopt, use or exhibit the titles "architect", "registered architect", "project architect", "consulting architect" or any other term of similar description; or

(d) Do anything likely to lead persons to infer that he is a registered architect.

(2) Any person who contravenes the provisions of subsection (1) shall be guilty of an offence and shall be liable upon conviction to a fine not exceeding one hundred thousand penalty units or to imprisonment for a term not exceeding twelve months, or to both.

(3)   Where an offence under subsection (2) is committed by a body corporate, every director and manager of the body corporate shall be deemed to have committed the offence, unless the manager or director proves that the offence was committed without his knowledge or consent.

(4)   Where a company does any act which if done by an individual would be an offence under subsection (2), every partner in that company shall be deemed to have committed the offence, unless he proves that the offence was committed without his knowledge or consent.

Offences relating to registration (Section 36)

(1)   A person shall be guilty of an offence if he-

    (a)   Makes or causes to be made an unauthorised entry, alteration or erasure in a register, practising certificate, or in any copy thereof; or

    (b)   Procures or attempts to procure for himself or any other person a practising certificate by means of fraud, misrepresentation or concealment of any material fact.

(2)   A person guilty of an offence under subsection (1) shall be liable, upon conviction, to a fine not exceeding one hundred thousand penalty units or to

imprisonment for a term not exceeding twelve months, or to both.

Urban and Regional Planners Act

The Urban and Regional Planners Act No. 4 of 2011 (hereinafter referred to as the *"Planners Act")* is a statute that establishes the Zambia Institute of Planners (ZIP) as well as provide for its functions; provide for the registration of planners and planning companies and regulate their professional conduct. [11]By section 2 of the Act, a *"planner"* means a person with special knowledge of urban designing, the environmental, social, economic and political issues with the spatial approach to problem solving acquired through planning education and experience. *"Planning"* means an area of expertise which involves the initiation and management of change in the built, socioeconomic, and natural environment across a spectrum of areas, ranging from urban to rural areas delineated at different geographic scales to provide and utilise services, further human development and sustain the environment.

The ZIP is established under section 3 of the Act which clothes it with statutory functions that include among others the following:

(a) Promote the spatial, aesthetic, economic and social development of urban and rural areas in the best interest of the community;

---

[11] Preamble to the Act

(b) Register planners and planning companies and regulate their professional conduct;

(c) Register students of planning;

(d) Develop, promote, maintain and improve appropriate standards of qualification in the planning profession;

(e) Develop, promote and enforce internationally comparable planning practice standards in Zambia;

(f) Investigate allegations of professional misconduct and impose such sanctions as may be necessary;

(g) Advise the government on matters relating to the planning profession;

(h) Promote the general advancement of planners and allied professionals for the improvement of the quality of life;

(i) Maintain and improve the standards of conduct and learning of planning and allied professions in Zambia;

(j) Facilitate the acquisition of knowledge by planners through the establishment of technical libraries, and the provision of monetary grants, books, apparatus and any other facilities necessary to achieve that end;

(k) Hold meetings of the institute for the reading and discussion of papers of professional interest to make awards to authors of papers of special merit and to arrange for other activities of interest or benefit to planners;

(l) Raise the character and status of the planners and allied professions to promote honourable and good practice and increase the confidence of the community in planners and allied professionals;

(m) Promote, protect and advance the general interests of planners and those engaged and interested in the planning field;

(n) Provide a forum for the communication and interchange of views on matters relating to planning and disseminate these views to the public;

(o) In collaboration with the disaster management unit, investigate and monitor national emergencies or disasters or any other matter of public concern caused by, or likely to be caused by planning services, and recommend appropriate preventive, rehabilitative or other measures;

(p) Represent, protect and assist planners with regard to their conditions of practice, remuneration or otherwise;

(q) Establish and maintain good relations with—

Other professional institutes and associations in Zambia; Other educational and scientific bodies in Zambia which have an interest in the planning profession and the education of planners in Zambia; or Similar institutions, associations or bodies in other countries; and

(r) Do all such other things as are necessary or incidental to the performance of its functions under [the] Act.[12]

The management and control of the affairs of the Institute is reposed in the Council of the Institute as provided for under section 8 of the Act. It is also the duty of the Council to register planners and planning companies.[13] The functions of the Council as set down under section 9 of the Act which are to:

(a) Perform all the functions of the Institute;

(b) Accredit planning educational institutions;

(c) Take such steps as may be considered necessary for the protection of the public and the improvement of standards of service rendered by planners;

---

[12] Section 4
[13] Sections 15 and 17; section 2 defines a *"planning firm"* to mean a statutory corporation, a company, a partnership, an association or other body, corporate or unincorporate, that provides a service through the application of planning skills and knowledge. On another hand, the registration of students of planning is done by the Institute and not the Council as per section 20 of the Act.

(d) Promote an understanding of professional ethics amongst the planners and create awareness of the importance of protecting the environment against unsound planning practices;

(e) Ensure that the rules and guidelines for professional ethics developed by the Institute are responsive to the expectations of business institutions, the public and those who rely on planning work;

(f) Participate in the development of international planning practice standard setting;

(g) Make recommendations affecting, or relating to, the planning profession to the general meeting of the Institute; and

(h) Promote continuing professional development among planners.

Offences under the Planners Act

Prohibition of person practising without registration (Section 13)

(1) A person shall not practise as a planner unless that person is registered as a Member under the constitution of the Institute.

(2) A person who contravenes subsection (1) commits an offence and is liable, upon conviction, to a fine not exceeding five hundred thousand penalty units or to

imprisonment for a period not exceeding five years, or to both.

Prohibition of planning firm practising without registration (Section 16)

(1)   A planning firm shall not provide any planning service or undertake any planning work unless that planning firm is registered in accordance with this Act.

(2)   A planning firm that contravenes subsection (1) commits an offence and is liable, upon conviction, to a fine not exceeding one million penalty units.

Disqualification from registration (Section 19)

(1)   A person shall not qualify for registration as a planner under this Act if the person

   (a) Has been convicted of an offence involving fraud or dishonesty under this Act or any other law;

   (b) Has been declared to be of unsound mind under any law in force in Zambia;

   (c) Is an undischarged bankrupt; or

   (d) Has been found, by the Disciplinary Committee, to be guilty of professional misconduct.

Cancellation of registration (Section 22)

(1) The Council shall cancel the registration of a planner, a planning firm or planning student where—

(a) The Council has reasonable grounds to believe that the registration was obtained through fraud, misrepresentation or concealment of any material fact;

(b) The planner or planning company is found guilty of professional misconduct under this Act or the Code of Ethics;

(c) The period for which the registration of the planner, planning firm or planning student was issued has lapsed;

(d) The planner, planning firm or planning student is convicted of an offence under any law; or

(e) Since the registration, circumstances have arisen disqualifying the planner, planning firm, or planning student from registration.

(2) The Council shall, before cancelling the registration under subsection (1), give the planner, planning company or planning student an opportunity to be heard.

(3) The Council may, before cancelling the registration of a planner, planning company or planning student, suspend the planner, planning firm or planning

student for such period and on such terms and conditions as the Council may determine.

(4) Where the Council cancels a certificate of registration under this section, the name of the planner, planning company or planning student shall not be restored except on such conditions as may be prescribed by the Council and upon payment of the prescribed fee.

Prohibition of practice without practising certificate (Section 23)

(1) A person shall not practise as a planner unless that person holds a practising certificate issued by the Council under this Act.

(2) A person who contravenes subsection (1) commits an offence and is liable, upon conviction, to a fine not exceeding five hundred thousand penalty units or to imprisonment for a period not exceeding five years, or to both.

Cancellation of practising certificate (Section 28)

(1) The Council shall cancel a practising certificate if the holder—

(a) Is found guilty of any professional misconduct;

(b) Is declared to be of unsound mind;

(c) Is an undischarged bankrupt;

(d) Contravenes the provisions of any law and is sentenced for a period exceeding six months;

(e) Obtained the practising certificate through fraud, misrepresentation or concealment of a material fact; or

(f) Commits an offence under this act or contravenes the code of ethics.

(2) Where a certificate of registration is cancelled under this Act, the practising certificate held by the holder of the certificate of registration shall be void and shall be surrendered to the Council.

(3) The Council shall, before cancelling a practising certificate under this section, give the holder of the practising certificate an opportunity to be heard.

(4) The Council may, before cancelling the practising certificate of a planner, suspend the planner for such period and on such terms and conditions as the Council may determine.

Holding out as planner or planning company (Section 39)

(1) A person shall not, unless the person is registered as a planner or planning company under this Act

(a) Practise as, be employed as, offer planning services, be engaged as an agent of, or hold out to be, a planner or planning company;

(b) Adopt, use or exhibit the titles *"registered planner,"* *"registered planning company"*, or any other title or abbreviation of like description; or

(c) Do anything likely to lead persons to infer that the person is a registered planner or planning company.

(2) A person or body corporate shall not offer employment to a person requiring registration under this Act.

(3) A planner or planning company shall not permit the planner's or planning company's name to be used by a person who is not a registered planner or planning company.

(4) A person who contravenes subsection (1), (2) or (3) commits an offence and is liable, upon conviction, to a fine not exceeding five hundred thousand penalty units or to imprisonment for a period not exceeding five years, or to both.

(5) Where a planner or planning company commits an act which if done by an individual would be an offence under subsection (3), every partner in that company shall be deemed to have committed the offence unless the partner proves that the offence was committed without the partner's knowledge or consent.

Offences regarding registered planner or planning companies (Section 41)

(1) A person shall not—

(a) Make or cause to be made an unauthorised entry, alteration or erasure in the Register or a certified copy of an entry in the Register or a certificate of registration or another certificate issued under this Act;

(b) Impersonate or use the title of a registered planner or planning company while not registered as such under this Act;

(c) Procure, or attempt to procure, registration under this Act, by fraud, misrepresentation, or the concealment of a material fact; or

(d) Forge a certificate of registration or another certificate issued under this Act.

(2) A person who contravenes subsection (1) commits an offence and is liable, upon conviction, to a fine not exceeding seven hundred thousand penalty units or to imprisonment for a period not exceeding seven years, or to both.

Professional misconduct (Section 44)

A planner or planning company commits professional misconduct if the planner or planning company—

(a) Contravenes the provisions of this Act;

(b) Unlawfully discloses or uses to the advantage of the planner or planning company any information acquired in the practice of the planner or planning company;

(c) Engages in conduct that is dishonest, fraudulent or deceitful;

(d) Commits an offence under any other law;

(e) Engages in any conduct that is prejudicial to the planning profession or is likely to bring it into disrepute; or

(f) Breaches the Code of Ethics or encourages another planner or planning firm to breach or disregard the principles of the Code of Ethics.

General penalty (Section 57)

A person who contravenes a provision of this Act for which a specific penalty is not provided, is liable, upon conviction, to a fine not exceeding one hundred thousand penalty units or to imprisonment for a period not exceeding one year, or to both.

Offences by body corporate or unincorporate body (Section 58)

Where an offence under this Act is committed by a body corporate or an unincorporate body, every director or manager of the body corporate or an unincorporate body shall be liable, upon conviction, as if the director or manager had personally committed the offence, unless the director or manager proves to the satisfaction of the court that the act constituting the offence was done without the knowledge, consent or connivance of the director or manager or that the director or manager took reasonable steps to prevent the commission of the offence.

Valuation Surveyors Act

The Valuation Surveyors Act, Chapter 207 of the Laws of Zambia is an Act to provide for the registration of valuation surveyors.[14] The Act defines *"valuation surveyor"* to mean a person engaged in the business of valuation of land, whether as a private practitioner or as an employee or agent of some other person.[15] The registration of surveyors in this jurisdiction is the assignment reserved for the Valuation Surveyors Registration Board.[16]

Offences under the Valuation Surveyors Act

Prohibition of un-registered persons from practising (Section 3)

(1)   Notwithstanding the provisions of any other written law, no person, unless he is registered as a valuation surveyor, shall -

(a) Practise valuation surveying of land or use any name, title or style containing the word *"valuer"*, *"valuing"*, *"valuation"*, *"evaluator"*, *"evaluating"*, *"evaluation"*, *"appraiser"*, "appraising" or *"appraisal"*, or any other word implying his being in the business of valuation surveying;

---

[14] Preamble to the Act
[15] Section 2
[16] Section 4

(b) Provide a valuation of land for any fee, commission, reward, or any other consideration, pecuniary or otherwise.

(2) Any person who contravenes the provisions of subsection (1) shall be guilty of an offence and shall be liable on conviction to a fine not exceeding two thousand five hundred penalty units or to imprisonment for a period not exceeding one year, or to both.

Suspension of valuation surveyors (Section 12)

The Board may suspend the registration of any valuation surveyor or strike out of the register the name of any valuation surveyor who is found, after due inquiry by the Board, to have been guilty of professional misconduct.

Land Survey Act

The Land Survey Act, Chapter 188 of the Laws of Zambia is an Act passed by the Zambian parliament in 1960 to:

Make further and more comprehensive provisions for the registration and licensing of land surveyors; to provide for the manner in which land surveys shall be carried out and diagrams and plans connected therewith shall be prepared; to provide for the protection of survey beacons and other survey marks; to provide for the establishment and powers of a Survey

Control Board which will be responsible for the registration and licensing of land surveyors and for the exercise of disciplinary control over such surveyors.

This statute is a principal legislation for the licensing of land surveyors as per sections 8 and 9 of the Act. The same statute outlines the duties of land surveyors which include among others:

(a) Carry out every survey undertaken by him in such a manner as will ensure accurate results and in accordance with the provisions of this Act and any regulations in force thereunder;

(b) Be responsible to the Surveyor-General for the correctness of every survey carried out by such land surveyor or under his supervision and of every general plan and diagram which bears his signature;

(c) Deposit with the Surveyor-General, for the purpose of being permanently filed in the office of the Surveyor-General, such records as may be prescribed relative to every survey carried out by him after the commencement of this Act; and

(d) When required by the Surveyor-General, without delay correct in any survey carried out by such land surveyor after the commencement of this Act or in any work appertaining thereto, any error which is in excess of the prescribed limits of error and take such steps as may be necessary to ensure the amendment

48

of any diagram and general plan based on such incorrect survey and to adjust the position of any beacon he has placed in accordance with such incorrect survey.[17]

The Act also establishes the Survey Control Board under section 6 whose functions are to conduct examinations of and trial surveys by persons who desire to become land surveyors; to keep a register of land surveyors; to hear complaints and to take such disciplinary action as may be necessary against land surveyors in accordance with the provisions of this Act; to make recommendations to the Minister relating to the making of regulations under section forty; and generally to control and regulate the practice of the survey profession.[18]

Offences under the Land Survey Act

Offences by land surveyor (Section 11)

If a land surveyor, other than a Government surveyor –

(a) Signs, except as provided in section thirty-four, a general plan or diagram of any parcel of land in respect of which he has not carried out or personally supervised the whole of the survey and field operations and carefully examined and satisfied himself of the correctness of the entries in any field

---

[17] Section 10
[18] Section 7

book, and the calculations, working plans and other records in connection therewith, which may have been made by any other person; or

(b) Signs a defective general plan or diagram knowing it to be defective; or

(c) Repeatedly performs, through negligence or incompetence, defective surveys, or surveys to which adequate checks have not been applied; or

(d) Makes any entry in a field book, copy of a field book or other document which purports to have been derived from actual observation or measurement in the field when it was not in fact so derived; or

(e) Supplies erroneous information to the surveyor-general in connection with any survey, boundaries or beacons of land knowing it to be erroneous; or

(f) Is guilty of such improper conduct as, in the opinion of the board, renders him unfit to practise as a land surveyor;

The Board may impose upon him penalties prescribed in subsection (1) of section 13 as it thinks fit.

Unauthorised practice as surveyor (Section 14)

After the commencement of this Act, no person, except a land surveyor, shall-

(a) Perform any survey for the purpose of preparing any diagram or plan to be filed or registered in the

Registry or referred to in any manner whatsoever in any other document to be so filed or registered;

(b) Perform any survey affecting the delimitation of the boundaries or the location of the beacons of any parcel of land registered or to be registered in the Registry; or

(c) Hold himself out in any matter whatsoever as a land surveyor;

And any person who contravenes any provision of this section shall be guilty of an offence and liable to a fine not exceeding three thousand penalty units.

Quantity Surveyors Act

The Quantity Surveyors Act, Chapter 438 of the Laws of Zambia establishes the Quantity Surveyors Registration Board (QSRB) which body is responsible for the registration, enforcement of professional standards as well as discipline of quantity surveyors.[19]

ii. Operational Laws

Companies Act

The Companies Act No. 10 of 2017[20] is the principal legislation that deals with the registration of all forms of companies in Zambia. By this Act, persons may incorporate and register either a public or private

[19] See sections 3 and 5; Parts III and IV of the Act
[20] Hereinafter referred to as the "CA" or "CA 2017"

company.[21] According to section 364 (1) of the same Act, it is an offence to fail to comply with requirements of registration as stipulated under Part II, that is sections 6 to 21 of the Act, making one liable, on conviction, to a fine not exceeding one hundred thousand penalty units.[22] In summation, the Companies Act is an Act, among others, to:

> Provide for the incorporation, categorisation, management and administration of different types of companies; provide the procedure for the approval of company names, change of name and conversion of companies; provide for shareholders' rights and obligations, the conduct of meetings and the passing of resolutions by shareholders; to encourage transparency and high standards of corporate governance by providing for the functions and obligations of company secretaries and directors; provide for issue of shares, share capital requirements, procedures for alteration and reduction of share capital and disclosure requirements of companies; provide for the public issue of shares, the issue and registration of charges and debentures; incorporate financial reporting

---

[21] Section 12

[22] See Chapter 1 in Gates, R. B. (2018). Gates on Understanding Company Law: A Conceptual and Functional Approach. Lusaka: Reagan Blankfein Gates for a detailed discussion on the types of companies and procedure for incorporation and registration of companies in Zambia

provisions, maintenance of accounting records, and access to financial information of companies; provide for amalgamations; provide for the registration of foreign companies doing business in Zambia; and provide for the deregistration of companies.[23]

Partnership Act

The Partnership Act of 1890 is an English Act which is applicable to Zambia by virtue of the British Acts Extension Act[24] and the English Law (Extent of Application) Act.[25] The Partnership Act is closely supported by the provisions of Registration of Business Names Act.[26] The Chapter on business associations will show the difference between a partnership and an incorporated entity.[27] However, it is important to note that the provisions of this Act will come in force and regulate a relationship between two or more persons in the absence of a partnership deed and if those persons are not incorporated into a separate legal entity called a company.

Environmental Management Act

The Environmental Management Act No. 12 of 2011 (hereinafter referred to as the "EMA") is an Act to

---

[23] Preamble to the Act
[24] Chapter 10 of the Laws of Zambia
[25] Chapter 11 of the Laws of Zambia
[26] No. 16 of 2011
[27] See Chapter 5 and 6

continue the existence of the Environmental Council and re-name it as the Zambia Environmental Management Agency; provide for integrated environmental management and the protection and conservation of the environment and the sustainable management and use of natural resources; provide for the preparation of the State of the Environment Report, environmental management strategies and other plans for environmental management and sustainable development; provide for the conduct of strategic environmental assessments of proposed policies, plans and programmes likely to have an impact on environmental management; provide for the prevention and control of pollution and environmental degradation; provide for public participation in environmental decision making and access to environmental information; establish the Environment Fund; provide for environmental audit and monitoring; facilitate the implementation of international environmental agreements and conventions to which Zambia is a party; and provide for matters connected with, or incidental to, the foregoing among others.[28]

This Act imposes a duty on all persons to protect the environment and goes further to provide for the right to a clean, safe and healthy environment.[29]This is achieved through environmental protection and pollution control strategies that have been provided under the Act which sees to it that the land, air, water and waste management

---

[28] Preamble to the Act
[29] Sections 5 and 4

systems are put in place by all who conduct activities that may endanger the environment.[30]

Offences under the EMA

Offences relating to hazardous waste materials, chemicals (Section 117)

A person who—

(a) Wilfully fails to undertake an environmental impact assessment contrary to the provisions of this Act;

(b) Fails to prepare and submit a project brief or an environmental impact assessment report as required under this Act; or

(c) Recklessly or fraudulently makes a false statement on an environmental impact assessment report submitted under this Act; commits an offence and is liable, upon conviction, to a fine not exceeding seven hundred thousand penalty units or to imprisonment for a period not exceeding seven years, or to both.

Offences relating to returns and records (Section 118)

A person who—

(a) Fails to keep a record required to be kept under this Act;

---

[30] Part IV

(b) Fails to submit a return required for purposes of this Act;

(c) Submits false or misleading information in any return; or

(d) Alters a record required under this Act; commits an offence and is liable, upon conviction, to a fine not exceeding three hundred thousand penalty units or to imprisonment for a period not exceeding three years, or to both.

Offences relating to environmental standards (Section 119)

A person who—

(a) Contravenes any environmental standards or guidelines established or prescribed under this Act;

(b) Contravenes a measure prescribed or ordered under this Act; or

(c) Uses the environmental or natural resources in a wasteful or destructive manner contrary to the prescribed standards, measures or guidelines;

Commits an offence and is liable, upon conviction, to a fine not exceeding seven hundred thousand penalty units or to imprisonment for a period not exceeding seven years, or to both.

Offences relating to biological diversity (Section 120)

A person who—

(a) Trades in any component of biological resources contrary to the provisions of this Act or any other written law;

(b) Unlawfully possesses any biological resources; or

(c) Unlawfully disturbs the habitat of a biological resource in contravention of this Act; commits an offence and is liable, upon conviction, to a fine not exceeding five hundred thousand penalty units or to imprisonment for a period not exceeding five years, or to both.

Offences relating to hazardous waste materials, chemicals (Section 121)

A person who—

(a) Fails to manage any hazardous waste and materials in accordance with this Act;

(b) Imports or exports any hazardous waste contrary to this Act;

(c) Knowingly mislabels any waste, pesticide, chemical, toxic substance or radio-active substance;

(d) Fails to manage any chemical or radio-active substance in accordance with this Act;

(e) Aids or abets illegal trafficking in hazardous waste, chemicals, toxic substances or pesticides;

(f) Disposes off any chemical contrary to this Act or hazardous waste within the Republic; or

(g) Withholds information or provides false information about the management of hazardous wastes, chemicals or radio-active substances;

Commits an offence and is liable, upon conviction, to a fine not exceeding one million penalty units, or to imprisonment for a period not exceeding ten years, or to both.

Offences relating to pesticides and toxic substances (Section 122)

(1) A person shall not—

(b) Detach, alter or destroy the labelling of a pesticide or toxic substance; or

(c) Use or dispose into the environment a pesticide or toxic substance in contravention of this act.

(2) A person shall not distribute, sell, offer for sale, store, import, export, transport, manufacture, change the composition of, or deal in any manner with any unregistered pesticide or toxic substance or without a licence.

(3) A person who contravenes this section commits an offence and is liable, upon conviction, to a fine not exceeding five hundred thousand penalty units or to imprisonment for a period not exceeding five years, or to both.

Offences relating to protected areas (Section 123)

A person who fails, neglects or refuses to comply with guidelines prescribed to regulate environmentally protected areas   commits an offence and is liable, upon conviction, to a fine not exceeding   three   hundred thousand penalty units or to imprisonment for a period not exceeding three years, or to both.

General penalty (Section 125)

(1)   A   person   who   pollutes   the   environment   or contravenes any provision of this Act for which no penalty is provided, is liable, upon conviction, to a fine not exceeding three hundred thousand penalty units or to imprisonment for a period not exceeding three years, or to both.

(2)   Except as otherwise specified in this Act, a person who is   convicted of an offence that is a continuing one, shall in addition to the penalty specified for the offence, be liable, upon conviction, to a further fine, for each day or part of a day on which the offence   continues—

(a) In the case of an individual, not exceeding five hundred penalty units per day on a   first conviction, and not   more   than   eight   hundred penalty   units   per   day   on   each   subsequent conviction; and

(b)   In the case of a body corporate or an unincorporate body, not exceeding one thousand penalty units per day on a first conviction, and not more than two thousand penalty units per day on each subsequent conviction.

(3) A court that convicts a person of an offence under this Act may suspend, revoke or amend any licence issued to that person under this Act.

Offences by body corporate or unincorporate body (Section 126)

Where an offence under this Act is committed by a body corporate or an unincorporate body, every director or manager of the body corporate or unincorporate body shall be liable, upon conviction, as if the director or manager had personally committed the offence, unless the director or manager proves to the satisfaction of the court that the act constituting the offence was done without the knowledge, consent or connivance of the director or manager or that the director or manager took reasonable steps to prevent the commission of the offence.

Urban and Regional Planning Act

The Urban and Regional Planning Act No. 3 of 2015[31] repealed and replaced most importantly the Town and Country Planning, Chapter 283 of the Laws of Zambia. The main highlight of the URPA is the establishment of National Planning Framework (NPF)[32] which is

[31] Hereinafter referred to as the "URPA"
[32] See section 16

administered by planning authorities among others.[33] It lays out the role of the Minister, Director responsible for planning and planning authorities in the implementation of the principles and standards for urban and regional planning as laid down under section 3 of the Act.[34]

The functions of the regional planning authorities are to coordinate the preparation of the regional development plan; advise and assist planning authorities within the region on the preparation of development plans to ensure compliance with the regional plan and the NPF; plan and co-ordinate the provision of infrastructure and facilities for the region; conduct research required for regional planning; recommend to the Minister such measures as may be necessary to comply with the principles and standards specified under section three; and carry out such other functions as are incidental and necessary to regional planning.[35] On the other hand, the functions of the provincial planning authorities are to:

(a) Monitor and advise on the planning, drafting, adoption and review of integrated development plans and local area plans;

(b) Facilitate the coordination and alignment of—

---

[33] Section 6
[34] Section 7 deals with the role of the Minister in planning; section 8 with Director of planning and section 9 with Regional planning authorities
[35] Section 10; section 13 establishes local authorities as local planning authorities; section 2 defines *"planning"* to mean the initiation and management of change in the built, socioeconomic and natural environment in, and across, a spectrum of sectors and urban and rural areas.

The integrated development plans of local planning authorities within the Province; and

The integrated development plans and local area plans of local planning authorities with the NPF and regional development plans;

(c) Take appropriate steps to resolve disputes or differences relating to the planning, drafting, adoption or review of integrated development plans and local area plans between local planning authorities in the Province, as may be prescribed, and refer the disputes that are not settled to the Minister;

(d) Assess integrated development plans and local area plans in terms of adherence to the principles, requirements, standards and planning guidelines provided for under the Act;

(e) Oversee all planning activities in the Province;

(f) Assist local authorities in planning, drafting, adopting, implementing and reviewing their integrated development plans and local area plans;

Planning permission (Section 49)

(1) A person shall not carry out any development on land, change the use of land or subdivide any land without planning permission.

(2)   A person who contravenes subsection (1) commits an offence and is liable, upon conviction, to a fine not exceeding three hundred penalty units.

(3)   A planning authority may, where a person carries out any development on any land, change the use of land or subdivides any land contrary to this Act, demolish the structure on the land without compensation.

(4)   A planning authority may, where a person changes the use of land contrary to its designated use as provided in an integrated development plan or local area plan approved under this Act, charge such fees in respect of the changed use as it may determine and direct that the land be restored to its original use.

(5)   Where planning permission is granted for a limited period, no further planning permission shall be required at the end of that period for the resumption of the purpose for which the land was lawfully used before the planning permission was granted.

(6)   Where an application for planning permission is for a specific part of the site in respect of which the application is made, it shall apply only to that part.

Offences and penalties (Section 71)

(1)   A person commits an offence under this Act if that person—

(a) Without lawful authority, uses or occupies any piece or parcel of land or building in an area to which this Act applies;

(b) Erects any building or structure in any area to which this Act applies without the prior approval of the planning authority within whose jurisdiction the land is situated; or

(c) Does or omits to do any act in contravention of any of the provisions of this Act.

(2) A person convicted of an offence under this Act is liable to a fine not exceeding two hundred thousand penalty units or to imprisonment for a period not exceeding two years, or to both.

Public Roads Act

The Public Roads Act No. 12 of 2002 is another important piece of legislation that professionals in the construction sector must be conversant with.[36] Most importantly, it is important that the professional either as an architect, engineer, surveyor or contractor must know what a public road, urban road and road reserve are as espoused under Part III of the Act. It is also important to be aware of the rights and responsibilities imposed on contractors during

---

[36] An Act to establish the Road Development Agency and to define its functions; to provide for the care, maintenance and construction of public roads in Zambia; to regulate maximum weights permissible for transmission on roads; and to provide for matters connected with and incidental to the foregoing as per Preamble to the Act

the care, maintenance and construction of roads as provided for under Part IV of the same Act.[37] Any person who commits an offence under this Act for which no special penalty is provided shall be liable, upon conviction, in the case of a first offence, to a fine not exceeding one thousand five hundred penalty units and, in case of a second or subsequent offence, to a fine not exceeding three thousand penalty units or to a fine not exceeding three thousand penalty units or to imprisonment for a term not exceeding three months, or both.[38]

Public Procurement Act

Contracting entities are expected to familiarize themselves with the public procurement process as envisaged in the Public Procurement Act No. 12 of 2008. It is imperative that these entities know the registration as well as bidding processes for public tenders and supply.[39] It is also important to be familiar with the offences and penalties under the same Act.[40]

---

[37] *"road"* means any highway, and any other road to which the public have access and any public place to which vehicles have access and any road in any residential area, whether access to it is restricted or not, which is part of a local authority area and includes any bridge, causeway, dam, ditch, drain, embankment, fence, ferry pontoon, ford, culvert or other work in the line of the road as per section 2 of the Act

[38] Section 77

[39] Parts V, VI and VII of the Act

[40] Part IX

Other Legislation

There are other pieces of legislation which are important in the construction sector some of which will be discussed in the chapters that follow. They are;

- The Anti-Gender Based Violence Act No. 1 of 2011
- The Citizens' Economic Empowerment Act No. 9 of 2006
- The Employment Code Act No. 3 of 2019
- The Gender Equity and Equality Act No. 22 of 2015
- The Industrial and Labour Relations Act, Chapter 269 of the Laws of Zambia
- The Mental Health Act No. 6 of 2019
- The Public Private Partnerships Act No. 14 of 2009
- Intellectual property laws
- Insolvency laws

CHAPTER

2

INSTITUTIONAL FRAMEWORK OF CONSTRUCTION LAW

2.0 Introduction

This Chapter examines the institutional framework in which Construction law operates. It will show which institutions professionals in the construction sector may interface. Specifically, this chapter will look at the courts of law, tribunals and disciplinary bodies since professional bodies in associations and institutes as well as their respective boards and councils have been dealt with in the preceding chapter.

2.1 Courts of law

The courts play an important role in the life of a professional in the construction sector. As can be seen from perusal of various pieces of legislation discussed above, whether enabling or regulatory, a time comes in the cycle of the construction sector when the profession interfaces with courts.

The first interface is with the engineers registered under the EIZ Act whose appeals from decisions of the Disciplinary Committee lies with the High Court.[41] Secondly, under the Valuation Surveyors Act appeals of decisions of the Board lie with the High Court.[42] Thirdly, appeals from the Disciplinary Committee under the Urban and Regional Planners Act lie with the High Court.[43]Fourthly, appeals from decisions made by the Survey Control Board under the Land Survey Act lie with the court as per section 13 (2) of the Act. Lastly, as an example again on the interface with the courts are provisions under the URPA. Section 62 of the URPA establishes the Planning Appeals Tribunal whose appeals lie with the Court of Appeal.[44]

2.2 Ministers

There are several provisions in various Acts of Parliament and subsidiary legislation that provide for administrative appeals to Ministers. It is always important to refer to the Statutory Instrument on *"Statutory functions, portfolios and composition of Government"* to know which Minister the Act is referring to.[45] Good examples are appeals under sections 27 and 34 of the ZIA Act which lie to the Minister. And by Government Gazette No. 836 of 2016 the portfolio for ZIA lies with the Minister responsible for Housing and

[41] Section 53
[42] Section 13
[43] Section 51
[44] Article 131 (1) (c) of the Constitution
[45] At the time of writing this book Government Gazette No. 836 of 2016 was in force

Infrastructure Development. Similarly, section 29 (1) of the Quantity Surveyors Act provides for appeals of the QSRB to lie with the Minister before the same can be escalated to the High Court.

2.3 Disciplinary Committees

Disciplinary Committees are a common feature of all legislation that creates professional bodies. In rare circumstances, complaints against professionals under a particular statute may be heard by a creature called other than a Disciplinary Committee. The sole purpose of Disciplinary Committees or whatever name they may be called is to enforce professional conduct and ethics by hearing complaints against those accused of abrogating either that professional body's Constitution or a Code of Conduct and indeed provisions of the enabling Act.

The following are examples of such creatures:

(i) Disciplinary Committee under the EIZ Act;[46]

(ii) Disciplinary Committee under the ZIA Act;[47]

(iii) Disciplinary Committee under the Urban and Regional Planners Act;[48]

(iv) Board under the Land Survey Act;[49]

---

[46] Established by section 48; functions conferred under section 49; and powers clothed on it by section 54
[47] Established by section 21; functions under section 22; and powers under section 23
[48] Established by section 46; functions under section 47; and powers under section 49

(v)   Board under the Valuation Surveyors Act;[50]and

(vi) Board under the Quantity Surveyors Act.[51]

2.4 Tribunals[52]

Tribunals are specialist judicial bodies which decide disputes in a particular area and sphere of law.[53] These judicial bodies are usually outside the hierarchy of the courts but may possess administrative or judicial functions.[54] The following are tribunals which may be relevant to the construction law domain:

(i)   Lands Tribunal established under the Lands Tribunal Act;[55]

(ii)   Planning Appeals Tribunal established under the URPA;

(iii) Rating Valuation Tribunal established under the Ratings Act;[56]

(iv)   Consumer Protection Tribunal established under the Competition and Consumer Protection Act;[57] and

(v)   Workers' Compensation Tribunal established under the Workers' Compensation Act.[58]

---

[49] Established by section 6; functions and powers under sections 7, 12 and 13
[50] Established by section 4; functions and powers under sections 5,9, 10 and 12
[51] Established by section 4; functions and powers under sections 5 and Part IV
[52] See Chapter 15 in Chirwa, J. (2020). Commentary on Public Law in Zambia: Law, Politics and Governance. Claremont: Juta and Company (Pty) Ltd
[53] id
[54] id
[55] No. 39 of 2010
[56] No. 12 of 1997
[57] No. 24 of 2010

CHAPTER

3

ALTERNATIVE DISPUTE RESOLUTION

3.0 Introduction

This Chapter examines the alternative dispute resolution mechanisms (ADRMs) which are available as surrogates to litigation in the courts of law. There are many alternatives to litigation but the most common ones in the construction industry are negotiation, mediation and arbitration. These provide better options to litigation which is complicated, time consuming and theoretically expensive. These ADRMs are not however, replacements of court litigation but merely alternatives.

3.1 Alternative Dispute Resolution

Alternative Dispute Resolution (ADR) consists of a group of flexible approaches to resolving disputes more quickly, friendlier and at a lower cost than going through the tedious path of court litigation which is adversarial in

[58] Act No. 10 of 1999

nature. The purpose and rationale for ADR may be summed as follows:

> It was developed as an alternative to the traditional dispute resolution mechanism, litigation, which had become costly, time consuming, did not give the parties control over the outcome of their disputes and was generally cumbersome. ADR refers to a variety of techniques for resolving disputes without resort to litigation in the courts. The concept behind the introduction of ADR methods was, inter alia, to reduce the delays and costs associated with litigation; to introduce relatively less formal methods of dispute resolution; to introduce consensual problem solving and empower individuals by enabling them to control the outcome of their dispute and develop dispute resolution mechanisms that would preserve personal and business relationships. ADR processes were thus intended to produce better outcomes all round.[59]

3.2 Negotiation

Negotiation is perhaps the most used form of ADR in the day-to-day course of business and our lives. It is a voluntary, unstructured and usually private process through

---

[59] Winnie Sithole Mwenda, 'Paradigms of Alternative Dispute Resolution and Justice Delivery in Zambia,' LLD Thesis (UNISA, 2006) at p. vi

which parties to a dispute can reach a consensual agreement for the resolution of their disagreement.[60] It is usually done by the parties themselves. However, parties may involve legal practitioners to negotiate on their behalf; acting as agents representing clients. The final agreement in both cases is made by the parties to a dispute themselves.[61]

3.3 Mediation

Mediation is a process in which a neutral third party, selected by the parties to a dispute, helps the parties in the settlement discussions and attempts to have the parties negotiate a resolution of the dispute.[62] It is a short-term, structured, task-oriented, participatory intervention process where disputing parties work with an impartial third party, the mediator, to negotiate towards a resolution of their conflict and it is the parties who are affected by a dispute who decide the outcome of that dispute.[63]

It is important to note that in this jurisdiction we have *court-annexed* mediation. This is opposed to the voluntary mediation discussed above as under court-annexed mediation it is the court, as opposed to the parties, that refer the dispute before it to mediation. Court-annexed mediation was introduced by the High Court (Amendment)

---

[60] Dada, T.O. (2006). General Principles of Law, 3rd edn, Lagos: T.O. Dada and Co. at p.530
[61] Nolan-Haley, J.M. (2008). Alternative Dispute Resolution. Minnesota: Thomson/West at p.15
[62] Goodman, A.H. (2005). Basic Skills for the New Mediator, 2nd edn., Rockville: Solomon Publications at p.20
[63] Nolan-Haley, J.M. (2008) at p.70

Rules of 1997[64] whereby a case already in court and deemed suitable for mediation is allocated to a trained mediator for mediation and if the mediation fails, the case is referred to court.[65]

3.4 Arbitration

Arbitration is the process in which parties to a dispute agree to submit the dispute to a third part, known as an arbitrator, and clothe that arbitrator with the authority and power to review the evidence and render a binding decision.[66] This is the most formalized alternative to litigation and is governed, as in the case of Zambia, by statute as found in the Arbitration Act No. 19 of 2000.

The starting point for arbitration is the *arbitration clause* which is inserted in a contract which contains an *arbitration agreement* whereby parties agree to submit themselves to arbitration in case of any dispute.[67] The second major issue is what is termed as *arbitrability* which focuses on whether a particular dispute is properly the subject of arbitration.[68] It must be noted that not all matters may be a subject of arbitration as other matters may be excluded from

---

[64] S.I. No. 71 of 1997

[65] See Joseph Chirwa, 'The Benefits of Alternative Dispute Resolution to a Country's Legal System and its extent of usage in Zambia: An Assessment,' LLB Thesis (Zambian Open University, 2014) under Chapter 3; see also Order XIX, Rule 3 (2) (g) of the High Court (Amendment) Rules, 2020 promulgated by S.I. No. 58 of 2020 which gives power to a Judge to refer a matter to mediation

[66] Goodman, A.H. (2004). Basic Skills for the New Arbitrator, 2nd edn., Rockville: Solomon Publications at p.19

[67] See section 9 of the Arbitration Act

[68] Nolan-Haley, J.M. (2008) at pp.166-167

arbitration by either policy or law. Section 6 of the Arbitration Act deals with the question of what issues may or may not be subject to arbitration. This provision states as follows:

(1) Subject to subsections (2) and (3), any dispute which the parties have agreed to submit to arbitration may be determined by arbitration.

(2) Disputes in respect of the following matters shall not be capable of determination by arbitration:

(a) An agreement that is contrary to public policy;

(b) A dispute which, in terms of any law, may not be determined by arbitration;

(c) A criminal matter or proceeding except insofar as permitted by written law or unless the court grants leave for the matter or proceeding to be determined by arbitration;

(d) A matrimonial cause;

(e) A matter incidental to a matrimonial cause, unless the court grants leave for the matter to be determined by arbitration;

(f) The determination of paternity, maternity or parentage of a person; or

(g) A matter affecting the interests of a minor or an individual under a legal incapacity, unless the minor or individual is represented by a competent person.

(3) The fact that a law confers jurisdiction on a court or other tribunal to determine any matter shall not, on that ground alone, be construed as preventing the matter from being determined by arbitration.

The following issues must be agreed in an arbitration agreement by parties beforehand in order to avoid a protracted process:

- Appointment of arbitrators
- Scope of arbitration
- Seat of arbitration
- Place of arbitration
- Governing law
- Fees for the arbitrator
- Fees for venue and conferences

CHAPTER

4

EMPLOYMENT AND LABOR RELATIONS

4.0 Introduction

This chapter examines employment and labour relations which are a core subject to professionals in the construction sector who may either be employers or employees. It also discusses the salient areas of employment law in Zambia noting that the field is broad to be compressed in a single chapter. Thus the chapter briefly discusses the nature of the employment contract, collective labour relations, discrimination, mental health, social security and occupational health and safety.

4.1 Employment contract

The law on employment contracts generally follows the established rules of the English contract law.[69] Thus, in order to find a contract of employment, certain basic elements of a contract must be met and these include offer and acceptance, consideration, intention to create legal

---

[69] See Chapter 7

relations and legality. In a nutshell, a contract of employment is a contract of service as opposed to a contract for services but also includes a contract of apprenticeship which may arise from an agreement expressed in writing, orally or from conduct.

Section 3 of the Employment Code Act[70]defines a contract of employment as an agreement establishing an employment relationship between an employer and an employee, whether express or implied, and if express, whether oral or in writing. The same provision defines *"employment relationship"* to mean:

> A relationship between employer and employee where work is carried out in accordance with instructions and under the control of an employer and may include—

> (a) The integration of the employee in the organisation of the undertaking where the work is— Performed solely or mainly for the benefit of an employer; and carried out personally by the employee; or

> (b) Work—

> Carried out within specific working hours or at an undertaking specified by the employer; Which is of a particular duration and has a certain permanency; That requires the employee's availability which requires the provision of tools, materials and

---

[70] No. 3 of 2019; hereinafter referred to as the "Code"

machinery by the employer; and that is remunerated and constitutes the employee's sole or principal source of income.[71]

The Employment Code goes further under Part III to state the important aspects of an employment contract in this jurisdiction. The first requirement is that all employment contracts in this jurisdiction must conform to the provisions of the code and the laws of Zambia.[72] The other pertinent issues relating to the contract of employment are as follows:

- The minimum contractual age is 15 (Section16);

- Requirement that contracts be in writing and contents thereof (Section 22 as read with section 23);

- The requirement of medical examination before employment (Section 17);

- Keeping of records in relation to oral contracts (Section 18 as read with sections 20 and 21);

- Permissible types of contracts (Section 19 as read with section 3)

---

[71] Section 3 of the Act goes on to define employee and employer as follows: *"employee"* means a person who, in return for wages, or commission, enters into a contract of employment and includes a casual employee and a person employed under a contract of apprenticeship made in accordance with the Apprenticeship Act, but does not include an independent contractor or a person engaged to perform piece work; *"employer"* means a person who, in return for service enters into a contract of employment and includes an agent, representative, foreman or manager of the person, who is placed in authority over the person employed.
[72] Section 15

- Submission of written contracts to Labour Office for attestation within 30 days of contract (Sections 25 and 26);

- Probation period of 3 months and not more (Section 27);

- Restrictions of transfer of contracts from one employer to another (Section 28 as read with section 29); and

- Contract of service, testimonial or reference (Section 59).

4.2 Collective labour relations

The law relating to collective labour and employment law is found in the Industrial and Labour Relations Act, Chapter 269 of the Laws of Zambia (hereinafter referred to as the "ILRA"). This is an Act that revises the law relating to trade unions, the Zambia Congress of Trade Unions, employers' associations, the Zambia Federation of Employers, recognition agreements and collective agreements, settlement of collective disputes, strikes, lockouts, essential services and the Tripartite Labour Consultative Council; the Industrial Relations Court.[73]

---

[73] It has to be noted that the Industrial Relations Court is now a Division of the High Court; Article 131 (2) of the Constitution provides that *"There are established, as divisions of the High Court, the Industrial Relations Court, Commercial Court, Family Court and Children's Court."*

Trade Unions[74]

A trade union is any group or organization of employees registered as a trade union under this Act whose principal objectives are the representation and promotion of interests of the employees and regulation of relations between employees and employers and includes a federation of trade unions.[75] A trade union may be formed by a group of employees not less than fifty in number or a lesser number as prescribed by the Minister responsible for labour.[76] The restrictions for one to be a member or after being a member to cease being a member are found under sections 4 (management) and 107 (essential service).

By virtue of Article 21 of the Constitution of Zambia and section 5 of the Industrial and Labour Relations Act (ILRA) all employees have a right to form and join a trade union of their choice as they enjoy the freedom of assembly and association.[77] Article 21 of the Constitution provides that:

(1)　Except with his own consent, no person shall be hindered in the enjoyment of his freedom of assembly and association, that is to say, his right to assemble freely and associate with other persons and in

---

[74] Excerpts from Chirwa, J. (2020). Essential Text on Local Government Law in Zambia. Claremont: Juta and Company (Pty) Ltd at pp. 117-119
[75] Section 3 of the Industrial and Labor Relations Act
[76] See section 9 of the Industrial and Labor Relations Act
[77] Zambia National Provident Fund Board v Rowlands Musukwa, SCZ Judgement No. 15 of 1995; Attorney-General and the Labor Commissioner v Zulu, Kamukwamba, Mundia, Muyangwa and Others [1995-1997] ZR 33 (SC)

particular to form or belong to any political party, trade union or other association for the protection of his interests.

(2) Nothing contained in or done under the authority of any law shall be held to be inconsistent with or in contravention of this Article to the extent that it is shown that the law in question makes provision–

(a) That is reasonably required in the interests of defence, public safety, public order, public morality or public health;

(b) That is reasonably required for the purpose of protecting the rights or freedoms of other persons;

(c) That imposes restrictions upon public officers; or

(d) For the registration of political parties or trade unions in a register established by or under a law and for imposing reasonable conditions relating to the procedure for entry on such register including conditions as to the minimum number of persons necessary to constitute a trade union qualified for registration; and except so far as that provision or, the thing done under the authority thereof as the case may be, is shown not to be reasonably justifiable in a democratic society.

Section 5 of the ILRA speaks in unison with the Constitution and the International Labour Organization (ILO) Conventions No. 87 of 1948[78] and No. 98 of 1949.[79] This section contains the rights that employees have in relation to collective bargaining and freedom of assembly and association. It provides, *inter alia,* that:

(1) Notwithstanding anything to the contrary contained in any other written law, and subject to this Act -

(a) Every employee shall, as between himself and his employer, have the following rights:
The right to take part in the formation of a trade union; The right to be a member of any trade union of choice;

(b) Every eligible employee shall have the following rights: The right, at any appropriate time, to take part in the activities of the trade union including any activities as, or with a view to becoming, an officer of the trade union and the right to seek election or accept appointment and, if elected or appointed, to hold office as such officer; and

The right to absent himself from work without leave of the employer for the sole purpose of taking part in the activities of the trade union, including any activities as, or with a view to becoming an

[78] Freedom of Association and Protection of the Right to Organize Convention which was ratified by Zambia on 2nd September, 1996
[79] Right to Organize and Collective Bargaining Convention which was also ratified by Zambia on 2nd September, 1996

officer of the trade union, and the leave of absence though applied for was unreasonably withheld by the employer

(2) No employer, or any person acting on his behalf shall-

(a) Prevent, dismiss, penalize or discriminate against or deter an employee from exercising any of the rights conferred on him by subsection (1);

(b) Refuse to engage a person, or dismiss, penalize or discriminate against any employee on the ground that, at the time of applying for an engagement, he was or was not a member of a trade union or of a particular trade union or other organization of employees; or

(c) Dismiss, penalize or discriminate against an employee on the grounds that such employee-

i. Has been or is a complainant or a witness or has given evidence in any proceedings, whether instituted against the employer before the Court or any other court;

ii. Is entitled to a reward, benefit or compensation against the association or the class of employers to which such employer belongs or against any other person, in consequence of a decision made by a Court in his favour or in favour of a trade union or the class of employees to which such employee belongs.

Employers' Organisations

The law relating to employers' organisations is found under Part IV of the ILRA. An employers' organisation refers to any group of employers registered under the ILRA.[80] The main objectives of such an organisation are the representation and promotion of employers' interests and regulation of relations between employers and employees, between employers and trade unions and between employers themselves. The rights of employers are found under section 37 which provides as follows:

(1) Subject to this Act -

(a) Employers shall have the right to participate in the formation of, and to join, an association and to participate in the lawful activities of such association;

(b) Nothing contained in any law shall prohibit any employer from being or becoming a member of any association lawfully in being or subject the employer to any penalty by reason of the employer's membership of any such association;

(c) No person shall impede, interfere with, or coerce, an employer in the exercise of his rights under this act;

No person shall subject an employer to any form of discrimination on the ground that the employer is or

---

[80] Sections 36 and 40

is not a member of any association; No person shall subject another person to any form of discrimination on the ground that the person holds office in an association; and no person shall impede or interfere with the lawful establishment administration or functioning of an association.

(2) No employee shall cease or suspend doing work for his employer on the ground that the employer -

(a) Is or is not a member or holds or does not hold office, in an association;

(b) Participates in the lawful activities of an association;

(c) Has appeared as a complainant or as a witness or has given evidence in any proceedings before the court or any other court; or

(d) Is or has become entitled to any advantage, award, benefit or compensation in consequence of a decision made by the court or any other court in favour of the employer, or in favour of an association or class or category of employers to which such employer belongs, either against such employee or against the trade union or class or category of employees to which such employee belongs or against any other person.

(3) Any person who contravenes any provisions of this section shall be guilty of an offence and shall be liable, upon conviction, to a fine not exceeding four hundred

penalty units and may be prohibited from holding office in a trade union for such period as the Court may determine.

Industrial Relations Court

The Industrial Relations Court is one of the divisions of the High Court as provided under Article 133 (2) of the Constitution. It is a specialized court to determine disputes arising from the ambit of labour and employment relations. It has original and exclusive jurisdiction in all industrial relations matters, involving the inquiry, adjudication and determination of collective disputes, interpretation of collective agreements and on any matter involving collective rights, obligations and privileges of employees, employers and representative organisations such as trade unions, employers' organisations among others.

4.3 Discrimination, Mental Health and HIV/AIDS

Discrimination under the laws of Zambia means different treatment to different persons attributable, wholly or mainly to their respective descriptions by race, tribe, sex, place of origin, marital status, political opinions colour or creed whereby persons of one such description are subjected to disabilities or restrictions to which persons of another such description are not made subject or are accorded privileges or advantages which are not accorded to persons of another such description.[81] By Article 23 (2) of the Constitution of Zambia it is forbidden to discriminate against employees based on the attributes or characteristics highlighted above. In a nutshell, discrimination is a failure to treat all persons equally where no reasonable distinction can be found between those favoured and those not favoured.

Discrimination under the Employment Code

The Employment Code proscribes discrimination in undertakings and the failure to adhere to the law subjects that offender to penal sanctions. Section 5 of the Code provides as follows:

(1) An employer shall promote equal opportunity in employment and eliminate discrimination in an undertaking.

(2) An employer shall not, in any employment policy or practice discriminate, directly or indirectly, against an employee or a prospective employee—

(a) On grounds of colour, nationality, tribe or place of origin, language, race, social origin, religion, belief, conscience political or other opinion, sex, gender, pregnancy, marital status, ethnicity, family responsibility, disability, status, health, culture or economic grounds; and

---

[81] Article 23 (3) of the Constitution of Zambia, Chapter 1 of the Laws of Zambia as amended by Act No. 18 of 1996

(b) In respect of recruitment, training, promotion, terms and conditions of employment, termination of employment or other matters arising out of the employment.

(3) For the purposes of this Act, it is not discrimination to—

(a) Take affirmative action measures consistent with the promotion of equality or the elimination of discrimination in an undertaking;

(b) Distinguish, exclude or prefer any person on the basis of an inherent requirement of a job;

(c) Restrict employment to citizens or in accordance with section 65; or

(d) Restrict access to limited categories of employment where it is necessary in the interest of state security.

(4) An employer shall pay an employee equal wages for work of equal value.

(5) A person who contravenes this section commits an offence and is liable, on conviction, to a fine not exceeding two hundred thousand penalty units.

Discrimination based on disability and mental health

Disability rights are protected under the Persons with Disabilities Act[82] while mental health issues are addressed

---

[82] Act No. 6 of 2012

by the Mental Health Act.[83] Most importantly, it is a requirement that all employers comply with the provisions of these statutes in relation to the employment of a person with a disability. Section 6 of the Mental Health Act provides that:

(1) A person shall not discriminate against a mental patient.

(2) A person shall not exploit or subject a mental patient to abusive, violent or degrading treatment including gender-based aspects.

(3) A person shall not call a mental patient by a derogatory name on account of a disability of that mental patient.[84]

On the same length, section 3 of the Persons with Disabilities Act provides the definitions of disability and discrimination in the context of persons with disability. Sections 35 to 39 of the Act provides for obligations of employers in relation to employment of persons with disabilities such as those relating to non-discrimination, promotion and welfare among others.

Discrimination under the ILRA

---

[83] Act No. 6 of 2019; Section 2 of the Mental Health Act defines mental health as *"the state of well-being in which a person realizes that person's potential to cope with the normal stresses of life, can work productively and is able to make a contribution to the person's community."*
[84] Section 94 of the Code provides for the obligation that employers have in providing medical attention and care to its employees

The ILRA also proscribes discrimination of employees based on their belonging to a trade union. Section 5 cited above proscribes discrimination in relation to an employee belonging to a trade union. Similarly, section 108 (1) of the Act provides that no employer shall terminate the services of an employee or impose any other penalty or disadvantage on any employee, on grounds of race, sex, marital status, religion, political opinion or affiliation, tribal extraction or social status of the employee.[85]

HIV/AIDS and Discrimination[86]

Discrimination and HIV/AIDS[87] go hand in hand especially in employment relations. Discrimination, has been defined in the Constitution to mean directly or indirectly treating a person differently on the basis of that person's birth, race, sex, origin, colour, age, disability, religion, conscience, belief, culture, language, tribe, pregnancy, *health*, or marital, ethnic, social or economic status.[88] Thus, as can be seen, the Constitution of Zambia is cognizant of the fact that discrimination can be based on the health of an individual among others.

---

[85] See Edith Solomon v Duncan Gilbey and Matheson (Z) Ltd, Complaint No. 17 of 1985 (sex and marital status); Judith Namposya v Hoechst (Z) Ltd, Complaint No. 62 of 1985 (sex); Grayson Kachikoti v Tap Building Products Ltd, Complaint No. 33 of 1982 (political affiliation); and Lloyd Mwiya Milupi v Zambia Seed Company Limited, Complaint No. 19 of 1982 (social status).

[86] Excerpted from Essential Text on Local Government Law in Zambia at pp.120-121

[87] HIV stands for Human Immunodeficiency Virus while AIDS stands for Acquired Immune Deficiency Syndrome and is caused by HIV

[88] Article 266

Article 23 of the Constitution provides, *inter alia*, that:

(1) Subject to clauses (6), (7) and (8), no person shall be treated in a discriminatory manner by any person acting by virtue of any written law or in the performance of the functions of any public office or any public authority.

(2) In this Article the expression *"discriminatory"* means, according different treatment to different persons attributable, wholly or mainly to their respective descriptions by race, tribe, sex, place of origin, marital status, political opinions colour or creed whereby persons of one such description are subjected to disabilities or restrictions to which persons of another such description are not made subject or are accorded privileges or advantages which are not accorded to persons of another such description.

Speaking on the same, section 5 of the Employment Code Act89 provides, inter alia, that:

(1) An employer shall promote equal opportunity in employment and eliminate discrimination in an undertaking.

(2) An employer shall not, in any employment policy or practice discriminate, directly or indirectly, against an employee or a prospective employee—

---

[89] See also section 108 of the Industrial and Labor Relations Act

(3) On grounds of colour, nationality, tribe or place of origin, language, race, social origin, religion, belief, conscience, political or other opinion, sex, gender, pregnancy, marital status, ethnicity, family responsibility, disability, status, health, culture or economic grounds; and

    (a) In respect of recruitment, training, promotion, terms and conditions of employment, termination of employment or other matters arising out of the employment.

(4) For the purposes of this Act, it is not discrimination to—

    (a) Take affirmative action measures consistent with the promotion of equality or the elimination of discrimination in an undertaking;

    (b) Distinguish, exclude or prefer any person on the basis of an inherent requirement of a job;

    (c) Restrict employment to citizens or in accordance with section 65; or

    (d) Restrict access to limited categories of employment where it is necessary in the interest of state security.

(5) An employer shall pay an employee equal wages for work of equal value.

Employees who may have HIV/AIDS are greatly subjected to discrimination in the workplace due to unfounded beliefs and fears towards the disease. Some of these beliefs and fears are culturally entrenched which require a robust education and sensitization campaign to root out. In the preface to an ILO Code on HIV/AIDS titled *"An ILO Code of Practice on HIV/AIDS and the World of Work"*, Former ILO Director-General Juan Somavia writes that:

> Beyond the suffering it imposes on individuals and their families, the epidemic is profoundly affecting the social and economic fabric of societies. HIV/AIDS is a major threat to the world of work: it is affecting the most productive segment of the labour force and reducing earnings, and it is imposing huge costs on enterprises in all sectors through declining productivity, increasing labour costs and loss of skills and experience. In addition, HIV/AIDS is affecting fundamental rights at work, particularly with respect to discrimination and stigmatization aimed at workers and people living with and affected by HIV/AIDS. The epidemic and its impact strike hardest at vulnerable groups including women and children, thereby increasing existing gender inequalities and exacerbating the problem of child labour.

4.4 Social security

Social security is a system in which people regularly pay the government (or private persons in form of schemes) money when in employment and receive payments from the government (or private persons in form of schemes) when they are unable to work as result of old age, ill-health or injury. It is the protection which society provides for its members, through a series of public measures, against the economic and social distress that would otherwise be caused by a stoppage or substantial reduction in earnings resulting from various social risks.[90] It envisages measures put in place by both state and non-state actors to protect individuals and households from income insecurity arising from various social and economic risks.[91]

Old age, death, invalidity and survivors' benefits[92]

The following is legislation that governs social security in respect of old age, death, invalidity and survivors' benefits:

- Constitution of Zambia(Article 187)
- Employment Code (Section 73)
- National Pension Scheme Authority Act[93]

---

[90] Mwenda, W.S. (2011). Employment Law in Zambia: Cases and Materials. Lusaka: UNZA Press at p.239; and Chungu, C. and Beele, E. (2018). Labour Law in Zambia: An Introduction. Claremont: Juta and Company (Pty) Ltd at p. 80

[91] id

[92] See Chapter XI in Mwenda, W.S. (2011); and Chapter 9 in Chungu, C. and Beele, E. (2020). Labour Law in Zambia: An Introduction, 2nd edn. Claremont: Juta and Company (Pty) Ltd

[93] Chapter 256 of the Laws of Zambia

- Public Service Pensions Act[94]

- Pension Scheme Regulation Act[95]

- Local Authorities Superannuation Fund Act[96]

Compensation and industrial safety[97]

The employee is also required to be compensated for injury suffered during employment. It must be noted that some jobs are inherently dangerous in that due to their nature employees tend to suffer injury which may impair them from ever working. Jobs in the construction industry may be said to fall into the category of those which are inherently dangerous and where employees are prone to injury and in some cases death. The main legislation in this regard is the Workers Compensation Act.[98] This Act establishes the Workers Compensation and Control Board and the fund thereof.[99] The gist of this law is to be a scheme for compensation of employees injured in the course of employment and it gives such an employee the right to be compensated.[100]

---

[94] No. 35 of 1996

[95] Chapter 255 of the Laws of Zambia; see also Amendment Act No. 27 of 2005

[96] Chapter 284 of the Laws of Zambia

[97] See Cane, P. (2006). Atiyah's Accidents, Compensation and the Law. Cambridge: Cambridge University Press on a general and detailed discussion on this subject matter

[98] Chapter 271 of the Laws of Zambia

[99] Part III, sections 10 -27; and Part IX, sections 104-109

[100] Part V, sections 51 to 64

4.5 Occupational health and safety[101]

Occupational Health and Safety (OHS) represent an area concerned with the safety, health and welfare of the people engaged in work or employment. It is an extensive multi-disciplinary field, invariably touching on issues related to scientific areas such as medicine – including physiology and toxicology – ergonomics, physics and chemistry as well as technology, economics and law.[102] Section 2 of the Occupational Health and Safety Act No. 36 of 2010 defines OHS as:

A service for the purpose of –

(a) Protecting employees against any health or safety hazard which may arise out of their work or the conditions in which the work is carried on;

(b) Contributing towards the employee's physical and mental adjustment, to the employees adaptation to their work and to their assignment to work for which they are suited; and

(c) Contributing to the establishment and maintenance of the highest possible degree of physical and mental wellbeing of employees.

OHS is important as it is directly linked to the employees' right to health and right to life as provided in the

---

[101] Excerpted from Chirwa, J. (2019). The Right to Life and Occupational Health and Safety in Zambia. Beau Bassin: Lambert Academic Publishing
[102] GRZ (2015). Report of the Auditor General on the Management of Occupational Safety and Health. Lusaka: OAG at p.17.

Constitution of Zambia.[103] According to Lord Wright in Wilsons & Clyde Coal Co. v English[104] the duty of care, which embraces OHS at common law, can be described in a threshold duty: to provide competent fellow employees, adequate plant and a safe system of work. Pitt[105] explains that each case must be tested against the general question – whether the employer took reasonable care for the employee's safety.

First, the competent fellow-employee was explained by Streatfield J., in Hudson v Ridge Manufacturing[106] when he opined that:

> Upon principle it seems to me that if, in fact, a fellow workman is not merely incompetent but, by his habitual conduct is likely to prove a source of danger to his fellow employees, a duty lies fairly and squarely on the employers to remove that source of danger.

Thus, under this principle, it is the duty of the employer to ensure only competent employees and those with no propensity to cause injury are assigned for work otherwise he/she will be liable for damages suffered. This also puts an obligation on the employer to train and equip the employees with skills to avoid injury in the workplace.

---

[103] Article 12
[104] (1938) A.C. 57
[105] Pitt, G. (2004). Employment Law, 5th edn., London: Sweet & Maxwell at pp.391-398
[106] [1957] 2 Q.B. 348

Second, the employer is responsible for ensuring that the workplace is not dangerous and that tools, machinery and other equipment used by employees are suitable for the task and is safe.[107] Third, it is up to the employer to ensure that the methods used to undertake the work, the system of supervision and general organization add up to a safe system of work.[108] This duty squarely lies on the employer, even where the worker is knowledgeable and experienced. Clearly, an important aspect of establishing a safe system of work is the provision of appropriate safety equipment; helmets, gloves, goggles, overalls, safety harnesses and guards among others.[109]

---

[107] Taylor v Rover [1966] 1 W.L.R. 1491
[108] General Cleaning Contractors v Christmas [1953] A.C. 180
[109] Pitt, G. (2004) at p. 395

CHAPTER

5

BUSINESS ASSOCIATIONS

5.0 Introduction

This Chapter will examine the various types of business associations in Zambia. Business associations are basically entities through which individuals conduct business. The most common forms of business associations applicable to most sectors including the construction industry are as follows: sole traders, partnerships, cooperative societies and companies.

5.1 Sole Traders

Sole trader or sole proprietorship is a form of business in which one person owns all the assets of the business in contrast to a partnership, trust or corporation and the sole trader is solely liable for all the debts and liabilities of the business.[110] This is basically a one person show and by its nature unlike other entities like companies, a sole trader business is merged with the person owning the business and as such there is no division between ownership and the

---

[110] Black's Law Dictionary at p.1392

management of the business. Sole proprietorships are generally regulated by the Registration of Business Name Act No. 16 of 2011 in as far as name clearance and registration of the respective business name is concerned.[111] Section 2 of the Act states that a "business" includes profession.

5.2 Partnerships

The law of partnerships in Zambia is governed by the Partnership Act of 1890 which is an English statute applicable to Zambia by virtue of Chapters 10 and 11 of the Laws of Zambia. This Act defines a partnership as; the relation which subsists between persons carrying on a business in common with a view of profit.[112] Persons who have entered into partnership with one another are for the purposes of the Partnership Act called collectively a firm, and the name under which their business is carried on is called the firm-name.[113] Section 2 of the Registration of Business Names Act speaks in unison when it states that firm means an unincorporate body of two or more individuals or one or more individuals and one or more corporations, or two or more corporations, who have entered into partnership with one another with a view to conduct business for profit.

---

[111] Section 2 of the Act states that *"business name"* means the name or style under which any business is carried on, whether in partnership or otherwise.
[112] Section 1 (1)
[113] Section 4 (1)

The authors of *Underhill's Principles of the Law of Partnership* examine the definition under section (1) and conclude that it raises three elements that must be proved that a partnership exists namely:[114]

(i)   A business[115]

(ii) Carried on in common[116]

(iii) With a view of profit.[117]

As a result of the commonality of purpose all partners are liable collectively and jointly for all the debts and contracted, liabilities incurred, and wrongs committed in the name of the firm.[118] It must be noted that each partner is an agent of not only the firm but of other partners as well.[119]

Partnership Deed

A partnership deed or deed of partnership is an agreement entered into by all partners in a firm detailing the rights and obligations of those partners. The partnership agreement,

---

[114] Ivamy, E.R.H (1975). Underhill's Principles of the Law of Partnership, 10th edn., London: Butterworths at pp.1-20

[115] See Keith Spicer, Ltd v Mansell [1970] 1 All ER 462; and Marconi's Wireless Telegraph Co., Ltd v Newman [1930] 2 KB 292

[116] See Re Fisher and Sons [1912] 2 KB 172

[117] Re Spanish Prospecting Co. Ltd [1911] 1 Ch. 92; Naval Colliery Co. Ltd v Inland Revenue Commissioners (1928) 138 LT 593; and Stekel v Ellice [1973] 1 All ER 465

[118] See sections 6 to 18 of the Partnership Act

[119] Section 5

as it is sometimes called, usually contains the following information:

- Name of the company
- Name of the business
- Place of the business
- The commencement of the partnership
- The duration of the partnership
- Capital contribution
- Bank account of the company and signatories thereto
- Outgoings and profits
- Management of the business
- Accounts and audit
- Dissolution
- Restriction clauses for retiring partners
- Death of partners
- Arbitration clauses

5.3 Cooperative Societies

A Cooperative society is any enterprise or organisation owned collectively by its members and managed collectively for social economic benefit and whose activities are not prohibited by law.[120] It is required by law that every Cooperative society is registered.[121] The liability of the members of a cooperative society for debts and liabilities of that cooperative society are limited to the amount, if any, unpaid on the shares respectively held by them, or on the membership fee, as the case may be.[122] A cooperative society is a body corporate with perpetual succession and a common seal hence it has separate legal personality from its members.[123] In this regard it may be stated that a cooperative society has limited liability and enjoys separate legal personality. The myth surrounding cooperative societies that these only apply to farmers must be dispelled forthwith as all industries including the construction sector can form them.[124]

5.4 Companies

The law governing companies in Zambia is found under the Companies Act of 2017. By section 2 of this Act, a company means an entity incorporated in accordance with this Act[125] and section 6 of the repealed Act.[126] This definition is not helpful either as it lacks the depth of a clear-cut and comprehensive legal definition. The authors of *Osborn's Concise Law Dictionary* define a company as an incorporated

---

[120] Section 2 of the Cooperatives Societies Act, Chapter 197 of the Laws of Zambia
[121] Part III of the Act
[122] Section 17
[123] Section 14
[124] See Chapter 4 in Malila, M. and Chungu, C. (2019). The Law of Business Associations in Zambia: An Introduction. Claremont: Juta and Company
[125] The Companies Act No. 10 of 2017
[126] Companies Act, Chapter 388 of the Laws of Zambia

body with a separate legal personality.[127] Furthermore a company is generally, an association of persons formed for the purpose of some business or undertaking carried on in the company's name.[128]Incorporation means the merging together to form a single whole; conferring legal personality upon an association of individuals or the holder of a certain office.[129]

Procedure for incorporation

The procedure is found under section 12 of the Companies Act. The first step is outside the CA but is found under the Registration of Business Names Act which is name clearance. The promoter(s) of a company are required to provide three names for clearance by the Registrar of Business Names.[130] Upon the names satisfying the provisions of the Act, the promoter will be required to pay a prescribed fee and the name will be cleared and reserved for the next stages under the CA.

The second stage is the application stage under section 12 of the CA as alluded to above. In terms of section 12 (3), the following shall accompany an application for incorporation of a company:[131]

---

[127] M, Woodley (ed.). (2005). Osborn's Concise Law Dictionary. London: Sweet & Maxwell at p. 18
[128] Id
[129] Ibid at p. 215
[130] See R v Registrar of Companies (1931) 2 KB 197; R v Registrar of Companies Ex parte Bowen[1914] 3 KB 1161; R v Registrar of Societies Ex parte More [1931] 2 KB 197 (CA); and Bowman v Secular Society (1917) AC 406
[131] Gates, R.B. (2018) at pp.11-19

- A copy of proposed Articles of the company, or statement that it has adopted the Standard Articles;

- Declaration of compliance made in accordance with section 13;

- Signed consent from each person named in the application as a director or secretary of the company;

- Declaration of guarantee by each subscriber, if the company is limited by guarantee;

- A statement of beneficial ownership which shall state, in respect of each beneficial owner—

    a) The full names;

    b) The date of birth;

    c) The nationality or nationalities;

    d) The country of residence;

    e) The residential address; and

    f) Any other particulars as maybe prescribed; and

- A declaration by the applicants that the particulars stated in accordance with paragraph (e) have been submitted to the Registrar with the knowledge of the individuals to whom the particulars relate.

If the application is accepted the Registrar issues a certificate of incorporation and certificate of share capital which two documents symbolizes the "birth" of that company and which serve as conclusive evidence that the said company has been registered.[132]

---

[132] Sections 14 to 17 of the CA

Attributes of incorporation

The world-over through many generations has opted to conduct business through incorporated companies mainly because of the advantages that come with incorporation. Zambia's Deputy Chief Justice Michael Musonda, SC once claimed that incorporated companies are said to be the most ingenious creation by humankind due to its attributes. The following are the attributes that come with incorporation:

(i) it has limited liability;[133]

(ii) It has perpetual succession;[134]

(iii) It can own property in its own name;[135]

(i) It can sue or be sued in its own name (separate legal personality);[136]

(ii) Rights and obligations of the company are distinct from those of the shareholders;[137]

(iii) Transferability of shares;[138] and

(iv) Borrowing (or raising capital).

---

[133] Salomon v Salomon and Co. (1897) ACC 22; Associated Chemicals Ltd v Hill & Delamain and Ellis & Co (1998) ZR 9

[134] Zambia Consolidated Copper Mines Plc. and Ndola Lime Ltd v Sikanyika and Others, SCZ Judgement No. 24 of 202

[135] Macaura v Northern Assurance Co. Ltd (1925) AC 619; Short v Treasury Commissioners (1948) 1 KB 122; and DPP v Gomez (1993) AC 442

[136] Section 22 of the CA; see also Tata Engineering and Locomotive Co. Ltd v State of Bihar 1965 AIR 40

[137] Lee v Lee's Air Farming Ltd (1961) AC 12; and Underwood v Bank of Liverpool (1924) 1 KB 775

[138] Section 188 (1) of the CA

CHAPTER

6

COMMERCIAL TRANSACTIONS

6.0 Introduction

This Chapter assesses the law relating to commercial transactions in Zambia. It looks at the nature of contract, the law relating to property relations, insurance, competition, and consumer protection as well as intellectual property and unfair trade practices. These are broad and independent fields of law hence they shall be looked at in a brief yet succinct approach.

6.1 Contract law

The law of contract in this jurisdiction is based on common law principles of contract as developed in England. The subject is broad but for the purposes of this discussion we shall restrict it by looking at the foundational concepts of contract law.

Definition and nature of a contract

A contract is an agreement giving rise to obligations which are enforced or recognized by law.[139] The factor which distinguishes contractual from other obligations is that they are based on the agreement of the contracting parties.[140] Simply put, a contract is an agreement though as will be seen later not all agreements are contracts unless certain elements are fulfilled.

The elements that one must prove for a contract to exist are offer, acceptance, consideration, and intention to create legal relations. It was held in the case of *George Lewis v Zimco Limited*[141] that a contract that does not contain these four elements is unenforceable and will leave a potential claimant without a remedy in the courts of law.

(i)   Offer

An offer is an expression of willingness to contract on specified terms, made with the intention that it is to become binding as soon as it is accepted by the person to whom it is addressed.[142] An offer must be distinguished from an invitation to treat in that an invitation to treat is merely an invitation to another party to make an offer

---

[139] Peel, E. (2011). Treitel's Law of Contract, 13th edn., London: Sweet and Maxwell at p.1
[140] id
[141] (1992) S.J. (S.C)
[142] Storer v Manchester CC [1974] 1 WLR 1403

111

which distinction was aptly enunciated in the celebrated case of *Carlill v Carbolic Smoke Ball Co.*[143]

Thus, the following may not amount to offers but constitute an invitation to treat:[144]

- Auction sales
- Display of goods
- Advertisements of unilateral contracts
- Advertisements of bilateral contracts
- Time tables and passenger tickets
- Tenders
- Sales of shares

(ii) Acceptance

An acceptance is a final and unqualified expression of assent to the terms of an offer.[145] An offer may be accepted by conduct, for example, by supplying goods in response to an offer to buy them;[146] or by beginning to render services in response to an offer in the form of a request for them.[147] It must be noted that for acceptance to be valid it must be

---

[143] [1892] EWCA Civ 1; see also Datec Electronic Holdings Ltd v United Parcels Service Ltd [2007] UKHL 23 in which the court held inter alia that a statement is not an offer if it in terms negatives the maker's intention to be bound on acceptance and that a statement may be an invitation to treat, although it contains the word *"offer"*.
[144] See Treitel's Law of Contract at pp.11-16
[145] Ibid at p.17
[146] See Harvey v Johnson (1848) 6 CB 295 at 305
[147] See The Kurnia Dewi [1997] 1 Lloyd's Rep. 533

unequivocal and unqualified in that a communication may fail to take effect as an acceptance because it attempts to vary the terms of an offer.[148] Such a qualified response to an offer may thus amount to a counter-offer.

(iii) Consideration

For a contract to be binding, consideration must accompany an offer and an acceptance as the last two alone are not sufficient. Lush J in the case of *Curie v Misa*[149] defined consideration as some right, interest, profit or benefit accruing to one party, or some forbearance, detriment, loss or responsibility given, suffered or undertaken by the other. Consideration is an act or forbearance of one party, or the promise thereof, is the price for which the promise of the other is bought, and the promise thus given for value is enforceable.[150]

The purpose of the requirement of consideration is to put some legal limits on the enforceability of agreements even where they are intended to be legally binding and are not vitiated by some factor such as mistake, misrepresentation, duress or illegality.[151] In the case of *Pillans v Van Mierop*[152] it was stated that the doctrine of consideration is based on reciprocity: *"something of value in the eye of the law"* which must be given for a promise in order to make it enforceable as a

---

[148] See Tinn v Hoffmann and Co (1873) 29 LT 271
[149] (1875) LR 10 Exch 153
[150] Dunlop v Selfridge case supra
[151] Treitel's Law of Contract at p.71
[152] (1765) 3 Burr. 1663

contract. Thus, an informal gratuitous promise therefore does not amount to a contract.[153]

Most importantly, it is a rule of law that consideration need not be adequate but must be sufficient. It is stated that under the doctrine of consideration, a promise has no contractual force unless some value has been paid for it.[154] In that regard, courts are not permitted to interfere with the bargain actually made by the parties meaning that courts do not, in general, ask whether adequate value has been given, or whether the agreement is harsh or one sided.[155] The court must only satisfy itself that there is sufficient consideration and not whether it is adequate.[156]

(iv) Intention to create legal relations

The parties must prove that they intended to be legally bound by the contents of their agreement. This is so because some agreements such as social and domestic arrangements may not be made with the intention of binding the parties to it. The example may be agreements between husband and wife as well as parents and children.[157] This is also true to some business and

---

[153] Re Hudson (1885) 54 LJ Ch. 811; Williams v Roffery Bros and Nicholls (Contractors) Ltd [1991] 1 QB 1 at 19

[154] Treitel's Law of Contract at pp.77-78

[155] id

[156] See Midland Bank and Trust Co Ltd v Green [1981] AC 513 at 532; Cheale v Kenward (1858) 3D. & J. 27; Townend v Toker (1866) LR 1 Ch. App. 446; and Tennent v Tennent (1870) LR 2 Sc. & Div. 6 at 9

[157] See Balfour v Balfour [1919] 2 KB 571; Merritt v Merritt [1970] 1 WLR 1211; Parker v Clarke [1960] 1 All ER 93; Jones v Padavatton [1969] 2 All ER 616 and Simpkins v Pays [1955] 3 All ER 10

commercial agreements which may only amount to mere puffs, free gifts or letters of intent (or comfort).[158]

Nature and purpose of contract

Every contract is an agreement but not every agreement is a contract. In order that an agreement constitutes a contract and becomes legally binding at law three conditions must be fulfilled:

(i)   The agreement must relate to the future conduct of the parties.

(ii)   The parties must intend that their agreement shall be legally binding and enforceable.

(iii) The agreement must not infringe any rule of law because an agreement designed to break the law or one that is contrary to public policy and morality is not a valid one and therefore unenforceable contract.

Thus, the main reason the law of contract exists is firstly to protect agreements; second, to ensure that parties to the agreement carry out their various promises made on that agreement; and third, to provide parties with remedies should the other contracting party fails to carry out what they undertook to do on that promise.

---

[158] See Rose and Frank Co v Crompton Bros Ltd [1925] AC 445; Edwards v Skyways [1964] 1 All ER 494; Carlill v Carbolic Smoke Ball case supra; Esso Petroleum Ltd v Customs and Excise Commissioners [1976] 1 WLR 1; Kleinwort Benson v Malaysia Mining Corporation [1989] 1 All ER 785; and Turriff Construction v Regalia Knitting Mills (1971) 22 EG 169

Concepts underlying contracts

The following are the main concepts that underlie the formation of contracts. These concepts are important as they play a part when courts are called on to construe the obligations and rights of parties to that contract in the event of breach of that agreement by one of the parties:

(i)   Freedom to contract (and not to contract)

The general view surrounding contracts is that persons of full capacity must be allowed to make contracts as they wished. Thus, it is the position of the law that parties are free to decide whether to enter into a contractual relationship or not.

(ii) Privity of contract

The doctrine of privity of contract means that as a general rule, only persons who are party to a contract may enforce the rights on that contract as persons who are not party to that contract have no rights on that contract and may rip no benefits from it or suffer detriment under it.[159] Put in another way, generally a contract only confers rights and imposes obligations arising under only on parties to that contract and it follows that third parties are strangers to that contract and may not be allowed to enforce it as they are not privy to that contract.[160] However, this rule has

---

[159] See Alder v Dickinson [1954] 3 All ER 396; and Scruttons v Midlands Silicones [1962] AC 446 (HL)
[160] See also Dunlop Tyre v Selfridge [1915] AC 847

exceptions that allow non-parties to sue on a contract to which they are not technically parties. These include agency[161] and collateral contracts[162] among others.

(iii) Capacity to contract

The general rule under common law is that every person is competent to bind himself or herself under a contract under concept freedom to contract (or not to contract). There are exceptions to this general rule in relation to minors and persons *non compos mentis* (persons of unsound mind). The current majority age is 18.[163]

Terms of contract

A contract typically has express and implied terms. Express terms are those specifically agreed on by the parties themselves whilst implied terms are those that are not expressly stated in the contract by the parties but which may be deduced from among others custom and practice, statute or by the courts by looking at the intention of the parties as well as the relationship between those parties.

---

[161] Scruttons v Midlands case supra

[162] Shanklin Pier v Detel Products [1951] 2KB 854

[163] See Wayne Barnes, 'Arrested Development: Rethinking the Contract Age of Majority for the Twenty-first Century Adolescent,' 76 MD. L.REV. 405 (2017); see Ryder v Wombell (1868) LR 4 Exch. 32; and Roberts v Gray (1913) 1 KB 520 on when people of minority age may enter into valid contracts

Illegal and unenforceable contracts

The maxim *ex turpi contractu actio non oritur* which simply translates that "from an immoral or iniquitous contract an action does not arise" guides illegal contracts. The law is that a contract founded upon an illegal or immoral consideration cannot be enforced by action. In the case of *Koufour v Greenberg*[164] the High Court for Zambia held that an agreement to commit a crime or perpetuate a tort is illegal and will not be enforced by the courts. In the same vein, in the case of *Itowala v Variety Bureau de Change*[165] the Supreme Court held that:

> A party cannot sue upon a contract if both knew that the purpose, the matter of performance and participation in the performance of the contract necessarily involved the commission of an act which to their knowledge is legally objectionable.[166]

The following contracts are illegal and thereby generally unenforceable:

- Agreements to commit an unlawful act.
- Agreements prejudicial to the interests of the state.
- Agreements to promote sexual immorality.

---

[164] (1982) ZR 30 (HC); see Mundanda v Mulwani and 2 Others (1987) ZR (SC) in which the Supreme Court stated that by way of exception that an illegal contract capable of being performed legally is enforceable
[165] (2001) ZR 96
[166] See also Bigos v Bousted [1951] 1 All ER 92

- Agreements with enemy aliens.
- Agreements hostile to friendly foreign states.
- Contracts in restraint of trade.

Checklist of cases on building contracts

- Musamba v Simpemba (Trading as Electrical and Building Contractors) (1978) ZR 175 (HC)
- Zambia Building and Civil Engineering and Contractors Ltd v Georgoupollos (1972) ZR 288 (HC)
- Chisanga v AC Builders Ltd (1976) ZR 198 (SC)
- Collett v Van Zyl Bros. Ltd (1966) ZR 65 (CA)
- Kariba North Bank Ltd v PFM Shewell (1985) ZR 150 (SC)
- Drake and Gorham (Z) Ltd v Energo Project Ltd (1990) ZR 58

6.2 Property relations

Property includes a vested or contingent right to, or interest in, or arising from—

(a) Land, permanent fixtures on, or improvements to, land;

(b) Goods or personal property;

(c) Intellectual property; or

(d) Money, choices in action or negotiable instruments.[167]

6.2.1   Land and real property

Land means any interest in land whether the land is virgin, bare or has improvements, but does not include any mining right as defined in the Mines and Minerals Act in respect of any land.[168] Land includes anything attached to the earth or permanently fastened to anything which is attached to the earth, but shall not include any mineral right in or under or in respect of any land.[169]

Ownership of land in Zambia

It must be noted that there is no such thing as ownership of land in an absolute sense or at any rate as all land is owned by the state and a person can merely hold land either directly or indirectly of the state on one of the various tenures. [170]Section 3 of the Lands Act states that all land in Zambia shall be vested absolutely in the President and shall be held by him in perpetuity for and on behalf of the people of Zambia. What a person can therefore "own"

---

[167] Article 266 of the Constitution
[168] Section 2 of the Lands Act, Chapter 184 of the Laws of Zambia
[169] Section 3 of the Interpretation and General Provisions Act, Chapter 2 of the Laws of Zambia
[170] Riddal, J.G. (1988). Introduction to Land Law, 4th edn., London: Butterworths at p.5

in this jurisdiction is merely an estate or interest in land for a defined duration.[171]

Limitations on ownership of land (common law)

The maxim *'cujus est solum, ejus, est usque et ad inferos'* which loosely translates as he or she who owns the soil is presumed to own everything 'up to the sky and down to the centre of the earth' applied when it came to land ownership at common law. This meant that an owner of land owned everything on that land including minerals and any chattel not the property of any known person which is found under or attached to the land.[172]However, there were the limitations recognized under that system implying that the following vested in the state still:

- Liability in tort for nuisance and under the *Rule in Rylands v Fletcher;*[173]

- Gold and silver (treasure trove);[174]

- Wild animals;

- Water rights;[175]and

- Air space.[176]

---

[171] Mudenda, F.S. (2007). Land Law in Zambia: Cases and Materials. Lusaka: UNZA Press at p.6

[172] Heyton, D. (1982). Megarry's Manual of the Law of Real Property, 6th edn., London: ELBS at p.550

[173] Rylands v Fletcher [1868] LR 3 HL 330 (escape of water); National Hotels Development Corp [T/A Fair View Hotel] v Motala [2002] ZR 39 (noise)

[174] Attorney-General v Trustees of British Museum [1903] 2 Ch. 598 at 608-611; Attorney-General of Duchy of Lancaster v Overton Ltd [1982] 1 All ER 524

[175] John Young and Co. v The Bankier Distillery Co. [1893] AC 691

Limitations on ownership of land (statutory)

There are also limitations imposed on the use and enjoyment of land in Zambia by various pieces of legislation. It must be remembered that all land is vested in the President as per section 2 of the Lands Act. The following are other statutory limitations:

- Section 2 of the Lands Act vests all land in the President and that land does not include any mining rights.

- Section 3 (1) and (2) of the Lands Act vests all minerals in the President;

- Section 3 of the Mines and Minerals Development Act[177] vests all minerals in the President.

- Section 3 of the Water Resources Management Act[178] vests all water in the President.

- Section 4 of the Warma Act provides for no ownership of water in its natural state by any person.

- The Urban and Regional Planning Act places control and regulation of development of land.

- The Public Health Act (Building Regulations) Act[179] places a requirement for obtaining of building permits before construction of any structure.

---

[176] Lord Bernstein of Leigh v Sky Views and General Ltd [1977] 2 All ER 902; Board of Works v United Telephone Co. [1884] 13 QBD 904
[177] Act No. 11 of 2015
[178] Act No. 21 of 2011 (hereinafter referred to as the "WARMA Act"
[179] Chapter 295 of the Laws of Zambia

- The Civil Aviation Act[180]provides restrictions on the erection of structures that may impede the free flow of air traffic.

- Section 3 of the he Zambia Wildlife Act[181] vests all wild animals in the President.

- Section 3 of the Land Acquisition Act[182]empowers the President whenever he/she is of the opinion that it is desirable or expedient in the interests of the Republic, to compulsorily acquire any property of any description.

- Section 3 of the Forests Act[183]vests all trees and forest produce in the President.

Institutions of land alienation in Zambia[184]

iii. The President

All land in Zambia vests absolutely in the President and shall be held by him or her in perpetuity for and on behalf of the people of Zambia. By President the law does not imply the individual office holder but rather the institution of presidency and the office of the president as individuals come and go but the highest office of the land remains. The president may only alienate land to Zambian citizens as a rule. Administrative Circular No. 1 of 1985 issued under

[180] No. 5 of 2016
[181] No. 14 of 2015
[182] Chapter 189 of the Laws of Zambia
[183] No. 4 of 2015
[184] See Chapter 3 in Lubumbe, J.K. (2017). Land Acquisition and Titling Procedures in Zambia. Ndola: Mission Press

the Ministry responsible for lands attests to this when it states as follows:

> Your attention is drawn to the fact that all land in Zambia is vested absolutely in His Excellency the President who holds it in perpetuity for and on behalf of the people of Zambia. The powers of His Excellency the President to administer land are spelt out in the various legislations some of which are; The Zambia (State Land and Reserves) Orders, 1928 to 1964, the Zambia (Trust Land) Orders, 1947 to 1964, the Zambia (Gwembe District) Orders, 1959 and 1964 and the Land (Conversion of Titles) Act No. 20 of 1975 as amended. His Excellency the President has delegated the day-to-day administration of land matters to the public officer for the time being holding the office or executing the duties of Commissioner of Lands. Under Statutory Instrument No. 7 of 1964 and Gazette Notice No. 1345 of 1975, the Commissioner of Lands is empowered by the President to make grants or dispositions of land to any person subject to the special or general directions of the Minister responsible for land matters.

The President may only alienate land to non-Zambians under the following exceptions:

- Where the non-Zambian is a permanent resident in the Republic of Zambia;

- Where the non-Zambian is an investor within the meaning of the Investment Act or any other law relating to the promotion of investment in Zambia;

- Where the non-Zambian has obtained the President's consent in writing under his hand;

- Where the non-Zambian is a company registered under the Companies Act, and less than twenty-five per centum of the issued shares are owned by non-Zambians;

- Where the non-Zambian is a statutory corporation created by an Act of Parliament;

- Where the non-Zambian is a co-operative society registered under the Co-operative Societies Act and less than twenty-five per centum of the members are non-Zambians;

- Where the non-Zambian is a body registered under the Land (Perpetual Succession) Act and is a non-profit making, charitable, religious, educational or philanthropic organisation or institution which is registered and is approved by the Minister for the purposes of this section;

- Where the interest or right in question arises out of a lease, sub-lease, or under-lease, for a period not exceeding five years, or a tenancy agreement;

- Where the interest or right in land is being inherited upon death or is being transferred under a right of survivorship or by operation of law;

- Where the non-Zambian is a Commercial Bank registered under the Companies Act and the Banking and Financial Services Act; or

- Where the non-Zambian is granted a concession or right under the National Parks and Wildlife Act.

iv. Commissioner of Lands

The office of the Commissioner of Lands (COL) is the head of the Department of Lands which is responsible for land allocation and alienation. The COL is not a constitutional nor statutory office but one created as a result of delegated functions in pursuant to the Statutory Functions Act, Chapter 4 of the Laws of Zambia. By this status quo, the COL performs all land allocation and alienation functions under the Lands Act and related legislation for and on behalf of the President.[185] Under Statutory Instrument No. 7 of 1964 and Gazette Notice No. 1345 of 1975, the Commissioner of Lands is empowered by the President to make grants or dispositions of land to any person subject to the special or general directions of the Minister responsible for land matters.

---

[185] Administrative Circular No 1, 1985

v. The Vice President

The office of the Vice President has the mandate of resettlement as one of its subjects under Gazette No. 836 of 2016 as well as previous gazettes on statutory functions, portfolios and composition of Government. Through the Department of Resettlement, the office of the Vice President may allocate land for the purposes of resettlement exercises.

vi. Local Authorities

A local authority means a council and its secretariat consisting of persons appointed by the Local Government Service Commission.[186] A council includes a city, municipal or town council.[187] Administrative Circular No 1 of 1985 provides that:

> Pursuant to the policy of decentralization and the principle of participatory democracy it was decided that District Councils should participate in the administration of land. To this effect, all District Councils will be responsible, for and on behalf of the Commissioner of Lands, in the processing of applications, selecting of suitable candidates and making recommendations as may be decided upon by them. Such recommendations will be invariably accepted unless in cases where it becomes apparent that

[186] Article 266 of the Constitution
[187] id

doing so would cause injustice to others or if a recommendation so made is contrary to national interest or public policy.

It must be borne in mind that as discussed in the previous Chapters, councils are designated as planning authorities under the URPA. It is for this reason that the councils were given the "agency" status in the allocation of land for and on behalf of the COL.

vii. Traditional Authorities

Traditional authorities, that is Chiefs, play a vital role in our national development agenda.[188] It is for this reason that the Lands Act recognizes the existence of customary tenure of land.[189] Thus, chiefs play a vital role in firstly, the allocation of customary land under that chief's jurisdiction and secondly, providing consent for conversion of customary tenure to leasehold. The consent letter by the Chief is addressed to the Council.[190]

---

[188] See Part XII of the Constitution
[189] See sections 3 (definition of customary tenure); section 7 (customary holdings to be recognized and to continue); and section 8 (conversion of customary tenure into leasehold tenure)
[190] See section 31 of the Lands Act as read with Statutory Instrument No. 89 of 1996 on the guidelines for converting customary tenure to leasehold tenure

6.2.2   Goods[191]

The dealing of goods in this jurisdiction is governed by the Sale of Goods Act of 1893 of England.[192] The SOGA defines "goods" to include all chattels personal other than things in action and money, and in Scotland all corporeal movables except money.[193] The term includes emblements, industrial growing crops, and things attached to or forming part of the land which are agreed to be severed before sale or under the contract of sale.[194]

Contract of Sale

A contract of sale of goods is a contract whereby the seller transfers or agrees to transfer the property in goods agreement to the buyer for a money consideration, called the price.[195] Contract of sale includes an agreement to sell as well as a sale.[196]The following are the major considerations of a contract of sale:

- It is first and foremost a contract between a seller and a buyer – offer, acceptance, sufficient consideration and intention to create legal relations ought to be present.

---

[191] See Chapter 3 in Malila, M. (2006). Commercial Law in Zambia: Cases and Materials. Lusaka: UNZA Press; and Atiyah, P.S. (1975). The Sale of Goods, 5th edn., London: Pitman
[192] Applicable to Zambia by virtue of Chapters 10 and 11 of the Laws of Zambia; Hereinafter referred to as the "SOGA"
[193] Section 62
[194] Id; see Settlement Trustees v Nuran (1970) EALR 570
[195] Section 1 (1)
[196] Section 62

- The subject matter of that contract is goods.

- The purpose of the contract is to transfer property in the goods.

- The transfer of the property in the goods is for money consideration called the price.[197]

- A contract of sale may be absolute or conditional.

- Where under a contract of sale the property in the goods is transferred from the seller to the buyer the contract is called a sale; but where the transfer of the property in the goods is to take place at a future time or subject to some condition thereafter to be fulfilled the contract is called an agreement to sell.

- An agreement to sell becomes a sale when the time elapse or the conditions are fulfilled subject to which the property in the goods is to be transferred.

- Capacity of the parties is as is a normal contract.[198]

Terms of a Contract of Sale

The normal principles of contract law determine the contents of a contract of sale. A statement will become a term of a sale of goods contract if the maker wants to be true and the maker intends it to be binding – mere representations may not be contractual terms.[199] Contractual terms may be classified as warranties or

---

[197] Keembe Estates Ltd v Galaunia Farms Ltd, SCZ Appeal No. 33 of 2003
[198] Section 2; see also Stocks v Wilson (1913) 2 KB 235; and Imperial Loan Co v Stone (1892) 1 QB 599
[199] Oscar Chess Ltd v Williams (1957) 1 WLR 370

conditions. The SOGA distinguishes between conditions and warranties not so much by reference to their *intrinsic nature* but rather reference to the buyer's remedies.[200] It recognizes that a condition is a more vital term the breach of which usually entitles the innocent party to treat the contract as *repudiated*. A warranty is a subsidiary term, the breach of which only entitles the innocent party to *damages*.[201]

Subject matter of the contract

The subject matter of a contract of sale is *goods*. This is a distinguishing characteristic of a contract of sale from other forms of contracts. Section 62 of the SOGA defines "goods" and excludes such things as land and things (choses) in action such as shares, trademarks, debts and negotiable instruments.

The status of the subject matter of the contract of sale

a. Existing and future goods

Section 5 (1) of the SOGA, goods subject of a contract of sale may be in existence (specific) or they may be future goods. Future goods include goods not yet in existence and goods in existence but not yet acquired by the seller.[202]

---

[200] section 11
[201] section 62; see Norman v Overseas Motor Transport (Tanganyika) Ltd (1959) EALR 131 (CAEA)
[202] Howell v Coupland (1876) 1 QBD 258

b. Ascertained and unascertained goods

Ascertained goods or specific goods are goods identified and agreed on after the contract of sale of goods is made.[203] Unascertained goods are those that are not identified and agreed on at the time the contract is made. They may be purely generic goods or unascertained goods from an identified bulk or source. Where there is a contract of sale of unascertained goods, no property in the goods is transferred to the buyer unless and until the goods are ascertained.[204]

Sale by non-owner

The transfer of property in the goods is the very essence of a contract of sale. The SOGA deliberately uses the term "property" to signify ownership rather than the physical chattel subject of the contract of sale. The rule *Nemo Dat Habeat Rule* which loosely translates as *"no one can give a better title than he himself possesses"* is instructive in these circumstances. Section 21 of the Act provides as follows:

> Subject to the provisions of this Act, where goods are sold by a person who is not the owner thereof, and who does not sell them under the authority or with the consent of the owner, the buyer acquires no better title to the goods than the seller had, unless the owner of the goods is

[203] Section 61
[204] Section 16; R v Zimba (1965) ALR 288)

by his conduct precluded from denying the seller's authority to sell.[205]

A non-owner may be able to pass good title to goods even if he or she may have none himself or herself, or if he or she has a defective title in the following ways:

(i)   Estoppel under section 21 (1) of the SOGA where it must be shown that either the owner represented that the seller was entitled to sell the goods, or that the owner was negligent in allowing the seller to sell the goods.[206]

(ii) Sale by court order[207]

(iii) Sale by agent[208]

(iv) Sale under voidable title[209]

(v)   Sale in market overt[210]

---

[205] Bishopsgate Motor Finance Corp. Ltd v Transport Brakes Ltd [1949] 1 KB 322; Clement H. Mweempe v Attorney-General and Interpol (2012) 2 ZR 155; and Power Equipment Ltd v Goldtronics Ltd and Barclays Bank PLC (1998/HP/1946)

[206] Eastern Distributors Ltd v Goldring (1957) 2 QB 600

[207] Rules of the Supreme Court of England, 1999 Edition, Order 29 Rule 4

[208] Section 61

[209] Section 23

[210] Section 22 (1) which provides that "Where goods are sold in market overt, according to the usage of the -market, the buyer acquires a good title to the goods, provided he buys them in good faith and without notice of any defect or want of title on the part of the seller." The term "market overt" applies only to an 'open' public and legally constituted market open between hours of sunrise and sunset and where goods for sale are openly or publicly displayed. See the cases of Lee v Bayes (1856) 18 CB 601 and Lonrho Cotton (Z) Ltd v Mukuba Textiles Ltd (2000) ZR 43

6.2.3 Intellectual property

Intellectual property is defined to include rights relating to:

(i) Literally, artistic and scientific works;

(ii) Performances of performing artists, phonograms and broadcasts;

(iii) Inventions in all human fields of endeavour;

(iv) Scientific discoveries;

(v) Industrial designs;

(vi) Trademarks, service marks and commercial names and designs; and

(vii) Protection against unfair competition; and all other rights resulting from intellectual activity in the industry, scientific, literary or artistic fields.[211] Intellectual property is a term that refers to the rights which result from intellectual creations in the industrial, scientific, literacy and artistic fields.[212] It basically comprises creations that result from the mind, the human intellect.[213]

Types of intellectual property[214]

Intellectual property is divided into two main branches namely: copyright and related rights and industrial property.

---

[211] Article 2 (viii) of the Convention Establishing the World Intellectual Property Organisation (WIPO) of 1967

[212] Kanja, G.M. (2006). Intellectual Property Law. Lusaka: UNZA Press at pp.1-2

[213] id

[214] Ibid at pp. 4-8

Copyright is a right granted for the protection of original literacy, dramatic, musical and artistic works; and other works such as computer programmes, compilations, sound recording, broadcasts and films, which result from the other's own intellectual creation. Performances of performing artists, phonograms and broadcasts are called related rights, that is, rights related to or neighbouring copyright. Related rights are rights that are granted to persons who present creative work to the public but who are not considered as creators of those works and these rights are granted to performers, phonogram and film producers, broadcasters and publishers. An industrial property covers inventions and industrial designs and includes trademarks, service marks, commercial names and designations, geographical indications and the protection against unfair competition. Unlike the protection of inventions which is the hallmark of industrial property, copyright law protects only the form of expressions of ideas and not the ideas themselves.

Conceptual framework

The broader field of intellectual property has with it several concepts that usually overlap and may be confusing to the layperson. The following are the major concepts and their definitions that may help in understanding the broader field of intellectual property law in the day-to-day activities of the construction industry:

- Copyright is a right granted for the protection of original literacy, dramatic, musical and artistic works; and other works such as computer programmes, compilations, sound recording, broadcasts and films, which result from the other's own intellectual creation. It is property right which subsists in original literary, musical, dramatic, artistic works and computer programmes; compilations; audio visual works; sound recordings; broadcasts; cable programmes; and typographical arrangements of published editions of literary works.[215]

- Trade mark is a sign which distinguishes the goods or services produced or provided by one enterprise or undertaking from those of another and these are closely associated with the business image, goodwill and reputation of a business. Trade mark is a mark used or proposed to be used in relation to goods for the purposes of indicating, so as to indicate, a connection in the course of trade between the goods and some person having the right either as proprietor or as registered user of the mark.[216] A mark includes a device, brand, heading, label, ticket, name, signature, word, letter, numeral or any combination of the same.[217]

---

[215] Section 7 of the Copyright and Performance Rights Act, Chapter 406 of the Laws of Zambia
[216] Section 2 (1) of the Trade Marks Act, Chapter 401 of the Laws of Zambia
[217] id

- Registered design is a monopoly right to protect the outward appearance of an article or a set of articles which have been manufactured and to which a design has been applied. It is features of shape, configuration, pattern or ornament applied to an article by any industrial process or means, being features which in the finished article appeal to and are judged solely by the eye.[218]

- Patent is a right granted for the protection of an invention,[219] which can be either a product or process that offers a new technical solution to a problem.[220] Patent means the letters patent granted for an invention which meets the requirements specified in section 15 of the Patents Act[221] and letters patent means an instrument that grants the exclusive rights of an invention to an individual or a corporation.[222]

Legislation concerned with intellectual property protection

The following are statutes that protect intellectual property, which is copyright and related rights as well as industrial property, in this jurisdiction:

---

[218] Section 2 of the Registered Designs Act, Chapter 402 of the Laws of Zambia
[219] Invention means a solution to a specific problem in a particular field of technology and includes a product or a service as per section 3 of the Patents Act No. 40 of 2016
[220] Kanja, G.M. (2006) at p. 6
[221] No. 40 of 2016
[222] Section 2

- Copyright and Performance Rights Act, Chapter 406 of the Laws of Zambia;

- Patents Act No. 40 of 2016;

- Registered Designs Act, Chapter 402 of the Laws of Zambia; and

- Trade Marks Act, Chapter 401 of the Laws of Zambia.

6.2.4 Commercial credit and securities

Commercial credit

Commercial credit is basically a facility to ensure that a business is advanced money for the performance of its contracts. Commercial credit may be in the form of loan credit, sale credit, fixed sum credit, overdrafts, and revolving credit among others. It may be given upon giving a personal undertaking to pay the debt on behalf of a company or indeed by use of security over property. The purpose of commercial credit is to access funding for a project whose funding is sourced from commercial banks or other lenders.

Commercial security

It is always a practice that for one to access funding from lenders they must provide security which may be personal in nature or security over property. There are many forms of securities given in the day-to-day world of lending, but the most common ones are discussed below.

viii.   Bonds and guarantees

Bonds and guarantees are usually used synonymously and correctly so. A guarantee or bond is some form of suretyship. It is a contract whereby one-person (guarantor) undertakes to be answerable to the other person (creditor) for the debt of another (principal debtor) if that person (principal debtor) defaults or fails to liquidate that debt. The contract requires three parties – the creditor, the principal debtor, and the guarantor (or surety). The guarantor's liability arises only after the principal debtor has failed to pay hence is described as secondary liability in contrast with the principal debtor whose liability is always primary. A condition precedent must be fulfilled before the guarantor can be liable on the bond.[223]

The guarantee can either be specific or continuing. It is specific if it only applies to a particular advance or credit or a specific loan. It is continuing if it extends to a series of transactions and is not exhausted by the first advance or credit hence not restricted to a particular advance or credit like a specific guarantee.[224]

---

[223] Paddington Churches Association v Technical and General Guarantee Co. Ltd 1999 BLR 244

[224] See generally the cases of African Banking Corp v Goldman Insurance Ltd 2007/HPC/0212; Zambia State Insurance Corp v Sasol Fertilizers (Z) Ltd Appeal No. 158 of 2001; and Intermarket Banking Corp. v Goldman Insurance Co. , Appeal No.125 of 2017

ix. Indemnity

This is a contract made between two parties one of whom undertakes to make good any loss suffered by the other in a given event, that is, one of the parties undertakes to indemnify the other against loss. The party who undertakes to make good the loss is called an indemnor (or indemnifier) while the party in whose favour the indemnity is made is called an indemnee. The most common form of an indemnity contract is insurance contracts which will be discussed in the succeeding chapters.[225]The indemnor is primarily liable to the indemnee and there is no secondary liability as in guarantee arrangements. The indemnor's liability continues in the principal contract, that is, between the indemnor and the person to whom the credit is extended and this liability extends even after the principal contract has been discharged.

x. Mortgages

A mortgage is simply to operate as a security and not a transfer of or lease of the estate of interest thereby created.[226] It is a conveyance of land or an assignment of chattels as security for the repayment of a debt or the discharge of some other obligation for which it is given. This security is redeemable on the payment or the discharge of some obligation. The transferor (or the borrower) is called the mortgagor and the transferee (or

---

[225] See Chapter 7

[226] Section 65 of the Lands and Deeds Registry Act, Chapter 185 of the Laws of Zambia

lender) is called the mortgagee. The principal money and interest on this money for which payment is secured are called mortgage money and the instrument (or document) by which the transfer is effected is called a mortgage deed.[227]

Legal and equitable mortgage

There are two types of mortgages namely legal and equitable mortgage. A legal mortgage is created in respect of a legal estate by deed of legal mortgage or legal charge while an equitable mortgage may be created by deposit of title deeds and by mortgage of an equitable interest in the land as opposed to a legal estate. There is a difference between the remedies of a legal mortgage (who is entitled to sell because he has a legal interest in the property) and an equitable mortgagee (who is not entitled to sell unless under a court order). In the case of *Kasabi Industries Ltd v Intermarket Banking Corp. Ltd*[228] it was held that equitable mortgagee only has an interest in the land and not a legal estate therefore cannot sell the property. It must be noted that the mortgagor is not allowed at law to sell the mortgaged property to him or herself in the event of

---

[227] See Kalusha Bwalya v Chadore Properties Ltd and Another, 2009/HPC/0294; Kasabi Industries Ltd v Intermarket Banking Corp. Ltd, Appeal No. 168 of 2009
[228] Appeal No. 168 of 2009

default.[229] It is also important to note that penal interest in addition to other interest triggered on default is illegal.[230]

xi. Debentures

A debenture is simply a document that creates or acknowledges a debt. It is a security given by companies and may contain either a fixed or a floating charge on a company's undertakings and property whether real or personal and whether present or future as security for a debt. The *Black's Law Dictionary* defines a debenture in the following ways: as long-term unsecured debt instrument, issued pursuant to an indenture; or promissory note or bond backed by the general credit and earnings history of a corporation and usually not secured by a mortgage or lien on any specific property.[231]

Floating charge

A floating charge is a charge or security which is not put into immediate operation but *"floats"* so that the company is allowed to use the assets that are secured. In the case of *Illingworth v Houldsworth*[232] it was held that the floating charge moves with the property it is intended to affect until some

---

[229] S. Brian Musonda (Receiver of First Merchant Bank Zambia Ltd in Receivership) v Hyper Foods Products Ltd and Others, SCZ Judgement No. 16 of 1999

[230] Union Bank Zambia Ltd v Southern Province Cooperative Marketing Union (1995-97) ZR 207; and Credit Africa Bank Ltd (In Liquidation) v John Dingani Mudenda (2003) ZR 66

[231] Black's Law Dictionary at p.401

[232] (1904) AC 355

event occurs or some act is done which causes it to settle and fasten about the charge within its reach. In *Re Yorkshire Woolcombers Association Ltd*[233] the court stated that a mortgage or charge by a company, which contains the following characteristics, is a floating charge:

(i) If it is a charge on a class of assets both present and future.

(ii) If that class is one which, in the ordinary course of business of the company will be changing from time to time.

(iii) If it is contemplated by the charge that, until some future step is taken by or on behalf of the mortgagee, the company may carry on its business in the ordinary way so far as concerns the particularly class asset so charged.

The case involving the *Attorney-General v Zambia Sugar Co. and Nakambala Estates Ltd*[234] is instructive on the nature of a floating charge. In summary to this discourse, the case states guides that a floating charge operates as an immediate and continuing charge on the property charged and has the effect of charging all the property in the hands of the borrower at the date of the charge. The court added that although a floating charge operates as an immediate and continuing charge on the property charged, nevertheless before it crystalizes the company has a free

---

[233] [1903] 2 Ch. D. 284
[234] (1977) ZR 273

143

hand to deal with and dispose of the property charged in the ordinary course of business. It may do so by way of sale, lease, exchange, specific mortgage or otherwise it deems most expedient.[235]

Fixed charge

A fixed charge (or specific charge) is fastened on ascertained or definite property or property capable of being ascertained and defined.[236] It prevents the company from disposing of the property without the consent of the holder of the charge.[237] A floating charge remains dormant until the undertaking charged ceases to be a going concern or until the person in whose favour the charge is created intervenes, e.g. when a receiver is appointed or the debtor defaults.[238] Then the floating charge will *"crystalize"* into a fixed charge which will bite on all the assets covered by the charge since normally a floating charge does not provide crystallization over part only of the assets to which it relates.[239] In the case of *Government Stock and Securities Investments Co. v Manila Railway Co.*[240] it was held that when a floating charge becomes a fixed charge, a company cannot thereafter deal with any part of the property so charged, except subject to the charge.

---

[235] See also Amiran v Agriflora (Z) Ltd (In Receivership) 2004/HP/0268; and Government Stock and Securities Investments Co. v Manila Railway Co. [1897] AC 81
[236] Illingworth v Houldsworth supra
[237] id
[238] Per Lord MacNaghten in Illingworth v Houldsworth supra
[239] Gower's Principles of Modern Company Law, 6th edn., at pp.367 quoted in id
[240] [1897] AC 81

A floating charge becomes a fixed charge in the following situations:

(i)   If the company is wound up.

(ii) If the company ceases to do business (that is it stops trading).

(iii) If a receiver is appointed.

(iv) If some event happens upon which the charge is to become a fixed charge and notice to that effect is given pursuant to the terms of the charge, e.g. In the debenture creating it.

6.3 Competition and consumer protection

Competition law

The law on competition in Zambia seeks to protect consumers by encouraging competition and fair trading by prohibiting and regulating monopolies and concentrations of economic power.[241] In addition, competition law seeks to strengthen the efficiency of production, and of the distribution of goods and services.[242] Other aspects of this area of the law are consumer welfare, freedom of trade and expanding the base of entrepreneurship.[243]

---

[241] CUTS, 'Enforcing Competition Law in Zambia', ZCA/CUTS (2002) at p.18
[242] id
[243] id

Consumer and Competition Protection Act

The Consumer and Consumer Protection Act[244] (hereinafter referred to as the "CCPA") is the main piece of legislation in as far as competition and consumer protection is concerned. The Preamble to the Act states the objectives of this CCPA in the following ways:

> An Act to continue the existence of the Zambia Competition Commission and re-name it as the Competition and Consumer Protection Commission; safeguard and promote competition; protect consumers against unfair trade practices; provide for the establishment of the Competition and Consumer Protection Tribunal; repeal and replace the Competition and Fair-Trading Act, 1994; and provide for matters connected with, or incidental to, the foregoing.

The main important bodies under this Act are the Competition and Consumer Protection Commission (CCPC)[245] and the Competition and Consumer Protection Tribunal (simply referred to under this Part as the Tribunal).[246] The CCPC has been given the mandate to among others:

(a) Review the operation of markets in Zambia and the conditions of competition in those markets;

---

[244] Act No. 24 of 2010
[245] Established under section 4
[246] Established under section 67

(b) Review the trading practices pursued by enterprises doing business in Zambia;

(c) Investigate and assess restrictive agreements, abuse of dominant positions and mergers;

(d) Investigate unfair trading practices and unfair contract terms and impose such sanctions as may be necessary;

(e) Undertake and publish general studies on the effectiveness of competition in individual sectors of the economy in Zambia and on matters of concern to consumers;

(f) Act as a primary advocate for competition and effective consumer protection in Zambia;

(g) Advise Government on laws affecting competition and consumer protection;

(h) Provide information for the guidance of consumers regarding their rights under this Act;

(i) Liaise and exchange information, knowledge and expertise with competition and consumer protection authorities in other countries;

(j) Advise the Minister on agreements relevant to competition and consumer protection and on any other matter relating to competition and consumer protection;

(k) Cooperate with and assist any association or body of persons to develop and promote the observance of standards of conduct for the purpose of ensuring compliance with the provisions of [the] Act; and

(l) Do all such acts and things as are necessary, incidental or conducive to the better carrying out of its functions under [the] Act.[247]

Consumer protection

Competition has a role in protecting consumers in that where it is effective, consumers will have a choice of products and services, and information in relation to these products and services which producers provide in seeking consumer patronage.[248] This, is believed by many, is achievable through government regulation aimed at extension and strength of the markets.[249]

Consumer protection is covered under Part VII of the CCPA and mainly concerns itself the following acts and practices:

(i) *Unfair trade practices* which occurs when a trading practice –

(a) Misleads consumers;

(b) Compromises the standard of honesty and good faith which an enterprise can reasonably be expected to meet; or

---

[247] See also section 54 on complaints by consumers
[248] Cranston, R. (1984). Consumer Protection and the Law, 2nd edn., London: Weidenfeld and Nicolson at p.18
[249] id

(c) Places pressure on consumers by use of harassment or coercion; and thereby distorts, or is likely to distort, the purchasing decisions of consumers.[250]

ii. *False or misleading representations* which occurs when a person or an enterprise:

(a) Falsely represents that-

- Any goods are of a particular standard, quality, value, grade, composition, style or model or have a particular history or previous use;

- Any services are of a particular standard, quality, value or grade;

- Any goods are new;

- A particular person has agreed to acquire goods or services; or

- Any goods or services have sponsorship, approval, affiliation, performance characteristics, accessories, uses or benefits that they do not have; or

- Makes a false or misleading representation concerning—

    i. The price of any goods or services;
    ii. The availability of facilities for the repair of any goods or of spare parts for goods;
    iii. The place of origin of any goods;
    iv. The need for any goods or services; or

---

[250] Sections 45 and 46

v. The existence, exclusion or effect of any
condition, warranty, guarantee, right or
remedy.[251]

iii. Display *of disclaimer* - an owner or occupier of a shop or
other trading premises shall not cause to be
displayed any sign or notice that purports to disclaim
any liability or deny any right that a consumer has
under this Act or any other written law.[252]

iv. *Supply of defective and unsuitable goods and services* - a person
or an enterprise shall not supply a consumer with
goods that are defective, not fit for the purpose for
which they are normally used or for the purpose that
the consumer indicated to the person or the
enterprise.[253]

v. *Product labelling* - a person or an enterprise shall not sell
any goods to consumers unless the goods conform
to the mandatory consumer product information
standard for the class of goods set by the Zambia
Bureau of Standards or other relevant competent
body.[254]

vi. *Price display* - A person or an enterprise shall not charge
a consumer more than the price indicated or
displayed on a product or service.[255]

---

[251] Section 47
[252] Section 48 (1)
[253] Section 49 (1)
[254] Section 50 (2)
[255] Section 51 (1)

vii. *Consumer product safety* - a person or an enterprise shall not sell any goods to consumers unless the goods conform to the mandatory safety standard for the class of goods set by the Zambia Bureau of Standards or other relevant competent body.[256]

viii. *Unfair contract terms* - in a contract between an enterprise and a consumer, the contract or a term of the contract shall be regarded as unfair if it causes a significant imbalance in the parties' rights and obligations arising under the contract, to the detriment of the consumer. An unfair contract or an unfair term of a contract between a consumer and an enterprise shall not be binding.[257]

Restrictive business and anti-competitive trade practice

Restrictive business and anti-competitive practices are prohibited under section 8 of the CCPA. The Act states that any category of agreement, decision or concerted practice which has as its object or effect, the prevention, restriction or distortion of competition to an appreciable extent in Zambia is anti-competitive and prohibited.[258] Part III of the Act criminalizes the following acts, conduct and practices termed 'restrictive business and anti-competitive':

---

[256] Section 52 (1)
[257] Section 53
[258] Section 8

- Bid rigging[259]

- Horizontal agreement prohibited *per se* as provided under section 9[260]

- Vertical agreement prohibited *per se* as provided under section 10[261]

- Concerted practice[262]

- Abuse of dominant position[263] as provided under section 16 whereby an enterprise is required to refrain from any act or conduct if, through abuse or acquisition of a dominant position of market power, the act or conduct limits access to markets or

---

[259] Section 3 defines bid rigging to mean a horizontal agreement between enterprises where - (a) one or more parties to the agreement agrees not to submit a bid in response to a call for bids; or (b) the parties to the agreement agree upon the price, terms or conditions of a bid to be submitted in response to a call for bids.

[260] horizontal agreement " means an agreement between enterprises each of which operates, for the purpose of the agreement, at the same level of the market and would normally be actual or potential competitors in that market as per section 3; "*per se*" in relation to a prohibited practice, means a practice which is prohibited in all circumstances so that it is not necessary for the Commission to demonstrate that it has anticompetitive effects as per section 3

[261] vertical agreement means an agreement between enterprises each of which operates, for the purposes of the agreement, at a different level of the production or distribution chain and relates to the conditions under which the parties may purchase, sell or resell certain goods or services as per section 3

[262] concerted practice" means a practice which involves some form of communication or coordination between competitors falling short of an actual agreement but which replaces their independent action and restricts or lessens competition between them as per section 3

[263] "*dominant position*" means a situation where an enterprise or a group of enterprises possesses such economic strength in a market as to make it possible for it to operate in that market, and to adjust prices or output, without effective constraint from competitors or potential competitors as per section 3

otherwise unduly restrains competition or has or is likely to have adverse effect on trade or the economy in general.[264]

---

[264] Section 16 (2) states that - For purposes of this Part, *"abuse of a dominant position"* includes— (a) imposing, directly or indirectly, unfair purchase or selling prices or other unfair trading conditions; (b) limiting or restricting production, market outlets or market access, investment, technical development or technological progress in a manner that affects competition; (c) applying dissimilar conditions to equivalent transactions with other trading parties; (d) making the conclusion of contracts subject to acceptance by other parties of supplementary conditions which by their nature or according to commercial usage have no connection with the subject matter of the contracts; (e) denying any person access to an essential facility; (f) charging an excessive price to the detriment of consumers; or (g) selling goods below their marginal or variable cost.

CHAPTER

7

INSURANCE

7.0 Introduction

This Chapter traverses the concept of insurance. It examines the nature and scope of insurance contracts, the elements of an insurance contract and how an insurance relationship is created. The Chapter also discusses various concepts in relation to insurance law such as insurable interest, subrogation and *uberrimae fidei* among others.

7.1 Nature and scope of insurance contract

A contract of insurance is an agreement entered into between the insurer and the insured in which the insurer agrees to compensate the insured or another beneficiary (third party) for losses arising as a result of specific risks.[265] In a contract of insurance one party undertakes, in return for a consideration paid by the other, to pay a sum of money or provide some equivalent benefit to the other if a specified event should happen, or when such an event

---

[265] Singer, R.M. (1980). Contemporary Business Law: Principles and Cases. New York: McGraw-Hill Book Co. at pp.22-31

should happen, or to make payments to the other until such an event should happen, the essence of the arrangement being that it is either uncertain whether, or uncertain when, that event will occur.[266]

Categories of contracts of insurance

Contracts of insurance may be divided into two broad categories namely, indemnity insurance and contingency insurance. Indemnity insurance is where the undertaking is to provide the insured with an indemnity against a possible future loss or liability, e.g. damage caused by fire, or a motorist's liability in tort to a third party who may be injured by his or her driving.[267] Contingency insurance happens where the promise is to pay a specified sum on the happening of a named event, e.g. a personal injury policy or a life policy.[268]

Parties to the contract of insurance

The contract of insurance or policy as it is commonly known will usually contain the following parties:

(i) *Policy holder-* this is the party (making or) taking out the policy and paying the premium.

(ii) *Insured (or policy holder or assured)* – this is the person whose life or property is insured.

---

[266] Sealy, L.S. and Hooley, R.J.A. (2009). Commercial Law: Text, Cases, and Materials, 4th edn., Oxford: Oxford University Press at p.1189
[267] id
[268] id

(iii) *Beneficiary* – this is the party to receive the proceeds of the policy.

(iv) *Insurer (or underwriter)* – this is the person who receives premiums and agrees to indemnify the other (insured) against loss resulting to him or her on the happening of certain events.

7.2 Concepts in insurance

7.2.1   Insurable interest

Insurable interest is a basic requirement of any contract of insurance unless it can be, and is, lawfully waived.[269] At a general level, this means that the party to the insurance contract who is the insured or policy holder must have a particular relationship with the subject matter of the insurance, whether that is a life or property or a liability to which he or she might be exposed.[270] The absence of the required relationship will render the contract illegal, void or simply unenforceable, or prevent a claim under it, depending on the type of insurance.[271]

---

[269] Birds, J. (2013). Birds' Modern Insurance Law, 9th edn., London: Sweet and Maxwell at p.41

[270] id

[271] See Macaura v Northern Assurance Co. [1925] AC 619; and Nyimba Investments Ltd v Nico Insurance Zambia Ltd, Selected Judgement No. 12 of 2017

7.2.2   Subrogation and indemnity[272]

An insurer cannot refuse to pay merely on the ground that the insured has a claim against a third party: the insured 'does not receive [money from the insurers] because of the accident, but because he or she has a made a contract providing for the contingency.[273] Equally, the third party cannot deny liability on the ground that the insurer has or will indemnify the insured.[274] Yet it is also the case that the insured cannot recover a sum greater than the loss suffered. The relationship between subrogation and indemnity is aptly stated by Brett LJ in the case of *Castellain v Preston*[275] when he opined that:

> *The very foundation, in my opinion, of every rule has which been applied to insurance law is this, namely, that the contract of insurance contained in a marine or fire policy is a contract of indemnity, and of indemnity only, and that this contract means that the assured, in case of a loss against which the policy has been made, shall be fully indemnified, but shall never be more than fully indemnified. That is the fundamental principle of insurance, and if ever a proposition is brought forward which is at variance with it, that is to say, which either will prevent the assured from obtaining a full indemnity or*

---

[272] Chapter 11 in Lowry, J. and Rawlings, P. (2005). Insurance Law: Doctrines and Principles. Oxford: Hart Publishing
[273] Per Pigott B. in Bradburn v The Great Western Railway Co. (1874) LR 10 Exch 1 at 3
[274] Parry v Cleaver [1970] AC 1
[275] (1883) 11 QBD 380 at 386

*will give to the assured more than a full indemnity, that
proposition must certainly be wrong.*

Subrogation is one means by which the insured is
prevented from obtaining more than a full indemnity. The
rights that insurers acquire from subrogation were
summarized by Brett LJ in the *Castellain case* above:

> *As between the underwriter and the assured the
> underwriter is entitled to the advantage of every right of
> the assured, whether such right consists in contract,
> fulfilled or unfulfilled, or in remedy for tort capable of
> being insisted on or already insisted on, or in any other
> right, whether by way of condition or otherwise, legal or
> equitable, which can be, or has been exercised or has
> accrued, and whether such right could or could not be
> enforced by the insurer in the name of the assured by the
> exercise or acquiring of which right or condition the loss
> against which the assured is insured, can be, or has been
> diminished.[276]*

7.2.3   Uberrimae fidei[277]

The principle of utmost good faith or the non-concealment
is another important principle governing insurance
contracts. To make insurance transactions fair for all parties
the law has elevated insurance contracts to the status of
contracts *uberrimae fidei*, contracts of the utmost good faith.
This requires that parties to the contract of insurance avoid

---

[276] At p.388
[277] Malila, M. (2006) at pp. 481-495

concealing any information material to the proposed insurance and that parties must not make misrepresentations that may mislead the other but must disclose all material facts without manipulation. Lord Mansfield in the case of *Carter v Boehm*[278] enunciated the underlying factors under this subject as follows:

> *Insurance is a contract upon speculation. The special facts upon which the contingent chance is to be computed lie most commonly in the knowledge of the insured only; the underwriter trusts his representations, and proceeds upon the confidence that he does not keep back any circumstances in his knowledge to mislead the underwriter into a belief that the circumstance does not exist and to induce him to estimate the risk as if it did not exist. The keeping back of such a circumstance is a fraud, and therefore the policy is void. Although the suppression should not happen through mistake, without fraudulent intention, yet still the underwriter is deceived, and the policy is void; because the risk is different from the risk understood and intended to be at the time of the agreement. Good faith forbids either party, by concealing what he/she privately knows to draw the other into his/her ignorance of that fact and his/her believing the contrary.*

In summary, the duty imposed by the principle of *uberrimae fidei* may be said to be as follows: firstly, a duty to disclose

---

[278] (1776) 3 Burr 1965

material facts; secondly, a duty not to misrepresent material facts; and thirdly, a duty not to make fraudulent claim.

7.3 Legislative and institutional framework

The main piece of legislation that governs insurance in this jurisdiction is the Insurance Act No. 11 of 1997 which repealed and replaced the Insurance Act, Chapter 392 of the Laws of Zambia. The Act is responsible for the regulation of the insurance market which is the mandate of the Pensions and Insurance Authority (PIA). The PIA is the regulatory and supervisory body for the pensions and insurance industry in Zambia. The PIA derives its mandate from the Pension Scheme Regulation Act No. 28 of 1996 as amended by Act No. 27 of 2005. In summary, the following are the laws that one must know as regards insurance:

- Insurance Act No. 11 of 1997
- Pension Scheme Regulation Act No. 28 of 1996
- Pension Scheme Regulation (Amendment) Act No. 27 of 2005
- National Health Insurance Act No. 2 of 2018

CHAPTER

8

LAW OF AGENCY

8.0 Introduction

This Chapter will examine the nature and scope of an agency relationship. Agency relationships are common in most industry set-ups and thus it is important that professionals in the construction sector are knowledgeable on how these relationships arise and how cease. It will also show that agency relationships may be recognized by statute as opposed to their creation by parties' agreement or conduct.

8.1 Agency relationship

The Latin legal term *"qui facit per alium facit per se"* which means the *"he who acts through another does the act himself"* is the fundamental term that summarizes the nature of the law of agency. To some extent, the maxim extends to liability of an employer for the act of an employee in terms of vicarious liability. Thus, the common law position is that *"he who can act for himself may also act through an agent"* in line with the maxim above. However, there are two exceptions to this position: first, where personal performance is required; and second, where the parties involved expressly or by necessary implication prohibit delegation.

Who is an agent?

Agency is the fiduciary relationship that arises when one person (a 'principal') manifests assent to another person (an 'agent') that the agent shall act on the principal's behalf and subject to the principal's control, and the agent manifests or otherwise consents to act.[279] It is the fiduciary relationship which exists between two persons, one of whom expressly or impliedly manifests assent that the other should act on his behalf so as to affect his relations with third parties, and the other of whom similarly manifests assent so to act or acts pursuant to the manifestation.[280] To bring the foregoing definitions into perspective, it can be stated that an agent is a person who has legal authority to bind another by entering into a contract with a third party on that other's behalf. The significant feature of the relationship is that an agent has power to bind his principal to a contractual relationship with a third party without the agent himself becoming a party to the contract. And as stated in the foregoing

[279] American Law Institute (2006). Restatement of the Law of Agency, 3rd edn., Minnesota: Thomson Reuters at para 1.01
[280] Reynolds, F. (2006). Bowstead and Reynolds on Agency, 18th edn., London: Sweet and Maxwell at art 1 (1)

Chapters, an agency relationship is an exception to the doctrine of privity of contract.

Creation of the agency relationship

The relationship of the principal and agent may be created in any one of the following ways. The first is through express appointment whereby the principal and agent agree expressly to enter an agency. The second is through implied appointment whereby the agency relationship may be imputed through the relationship of the parties, practice and the law such as directors and partners. It is important to note that agency relationships arising out of agreement will always be consensual but need not be contractual as guided in the case of *Yasuda Fire and Marine Insurance Co of Europe Ltd v Orion Marine Insurance Underwriting Agency Ltd.*[281] In this case, Coleman J opined as follows:

> *Although in modern commercial transactions agencies are almost founded upon a contract between principal and agent, there is no necessity for such a contract to exist. It is sufficient if there is consent by the principal to the exercise by the agent of authority and consent by the agent to his exercising such authority on behalf of the principal.*

The agreement between the principal and agent may be expressed orally, in writing or by deed (usually called a Power of Attorney). In general no formality is required as an agent may be appointed, as stated above, orally.

---

[281] [1995] QB 174

8.2 Types of agents

There is an endless list of agents who are used world-over as the use of agents allows principals to be in many places at a given time thereby expanding their businesses through the use of *"middlepersons"*. The following are examples of the types of agents commonly used:[282]

a. Auctioneers, who are agents for the seller, but may also be agents for the buyer for certain purposes;[283]

b. Directors, who are agents of the company when they act collectively as a Board of Directors;[284]

c. Partners, who are agents of the company and their other partners for the purpose of the business of the partnership;[285]

d. Solicitors and counsel, who are agents of their clients when, inter alia, they affect a compromise of matters connected with, but not merely collateral to, the litigation in question;[286]

---

[282] Sealy, L.S. and Hooley, R.J.A. (2009) at pp.103-105

[283] Hinde v Whitehouse (1806) 7 East 558

[284] See section 86 of the Companies Act No. 10 of 2017; Associated Chemicals Ltd v Hill & Delamain Zambia Ltd and Ellis & Co. (As a Law Firm), SCZ Judgement No. 2 of 1998

[285] See section 5 of the Partnership Act, 1890

[286] Waugh v HB Clifford & Sons Ltd [1982] Ch. 374

e. Sheriffs, acts not as agent of their employer, that is Judicial Service Commission, but of the party at whose instance the writ of *fieri facias* (writ of fifa);[287]

f. Tax collectors are agents of the tax authorities for the purposes of facilitating the collection of tax;[288]

g. Factors, who are in possession or control of the goods to be sold for their principal;[289]

h. Brokers, who negotiate and makes contracts between buyers and sellers of goods and services (e.g. stockbroker, insurance broker and credit-broker);[290]

i. *Del credere* agent, who in return for extra commission, undertake to indemnify the principal should the principal suffer loss as a result of the failure of a customer, introduced by the agent, to pay the purchase price of the goods sold, when the price is ascertained and due;[291]

j. Confirming houses, who usually act as an agent for an overseas buyer who wishes to import goods; and[292]

---

[287] See section 14 of the Sheriffs Act, Chapter 37 of the Laws of Zambia; see Attorney-General v E.B. Jones Machinists Ltd (2000) ZR 114

[288] See section 84 of Income Tax, Chapter 323 of the Laws of Zambia

[289] Baring v Corrie (1818) 2B & Aid 137; Stevens v Biller (1883) 25 Ch. D 31

[290] Baring v Corrie supra

[291] Morris v Cleasby (1816) 4 M & S 566; Thomas Gabriel & Sons v Churchill and Sim [1914] 3 KB 1272

[292] Sobell Industries Ltd v Cory Bros & Co [1955] 2 Lloyd's Rep 82; Anglo-African Shipping Co of New York Inc. v J Mortner Ltd [1962] 1 Lloyd's Rep 610

k. Commission agents, sometimes called commission merchants, contract with third parties as principals in their own name, although all contracts will be made by the agent on behalf of their principal.[293]

8.3 Duties and rights of an agent

The agency relationship brings with it rights as well as corresponding obligations on the part of the agent. The agent has certain rights that they must enjoy as a matter of right from the principal. But the truth is also that the agent has corresponding duties and obligations that they must discharge in order to enjoy those rights.

Duties of an agent

The case of *Armstrong v Jackson*[294] states that the position of principal and agent relationship gives rise to particular and onerous duties on the part of the agent and high standards required from the agent emanate from the fiduciary relationship between the agent's employer and himself. The following are the duties of an agent which in themselves are not exhaustive but merely projecting the most important ones so to say:

a. Duty to perform his (or her) undertaking

b. Duty to obey lawful instructions

c. Duty to exercise and show proper care and skill

---

[293] Robinson v Mollett (1875) LR 7 HL 802; Ireland v Livingston (1872) LR 5 HL 395

[294] (1917) 2 KBD 822 at 826

d. Duty to avoid a conflict of interest between the principal's interests and that agent's interest

e. Duty not to compete with principal

f. Duty not to make a secret profit

g. Duty not to accept or take bribes

h. Duty to indemnify the principal

i. Duty to account

j. Duty not to delegate

k. Duty not to disclose or cause to be disclosed confidential information

Rights of an agent

The agency relationship primarily brings to the fore three main rights namely: right to remuneration and compensation; right to reimbursement and indemnity; and the right to lien. Under the right to remuneration and compensation, the agent has a right to be paid his or her commission, salary or wages upon completion his or her assignment. The main gist of the agency relationship is for the agent to either make a commission or get salary or wages as the case maybe when the assignment completes, or the relationship is determined.[295] The right to reimbursement and compensation entitles the agent to recover reasonable and lawful expenses incurred by that agent in the execution of their duties on behalf of their principal. It is only fair and just that an agent is reimbursed

---

[295] See Way v Latilla (1973) All ER 759; and Coles v Enoch (1939)3 All ER 327

by his or her principal for all expenses and indemnified against all liabilities incurred by that agent while acting within the scope of his or her express or implied actual authority.[296] This is also the position when the agent exceeds his or her authority but that agent's unauthorised acts are subsequently ratified by that agent's principal.[297]Lastly, the agent has a right to a lien whereby the agent has a right to detain goods belonging to his principal until that agent is paid what he or she is owed by the principal in respect of those goods.[298] Thus, until his or her remuneration is paid or expenses and liabilities indemnified, the agent is allowed to hold on to the property of his or her principal.

8.4 Power of Attorney

A power of attorney (POA) is formal authority conferred by deed by one person on another to act as their attorney, or agent, or legal representative.[299] It is an instrument in writing whereby one person, as principal, appoints another as their agent and confers authority to perform certain specified acts or kinds of acts on behalf of that principal.[300]

---

[296] Rhodes v Fielder, Jones & Harrison (1919) 89 LJKB 159 KBD; see also Adams v Morgan & Co [1924] 1 KB 751
[297] See Barron v Fitzgerald (1840) 6 Bing NC 201
[298] See Taylor v Robinson (1818) 2 Moore CP 730; and Dixon v Stansfeld (1850) 10 CB 398
[299] Walker, D.M. (1980). The Oxford Companion to Law. Oxford: Clarendon Press at p. 974
[300] Black's Law Dictionary at p.1171

The powers conferred are set out in the deed and may be limited to one transaction or general and unlimited.[301]

Nature of power of attorney

A POA is an arrangement by which one person called the 'donor' gives another person called the 'attorney' or 'donee' authority to act on his or her behalf and name. The rules relating to the capacity to appoint an attorney are the same as those governing the capacity to enter into a contract and the general rule to contractual capacity is that a person concerned must be capable of understanding the nature and effect of the contract at the time it is created.[302] A POA is a contract of service and therefore binding on a minor if it is for the minor's benefit and in the case of persons who have mental incapacity and disorders is only binding if that person is understanding the terms of the instrument. It is a requirement that an instrument creating a POA must be executed as deed by the donor.[303]

---

[301] The Oxford Companion to Law at p. 974
[302] G (A) v G (T) (1970) 2 QB 643
[303] Attorney-General and Another v Ireen Mohingi Lemba (2008) ZR 215

3rd February, 2021

The Head of Procurement,
Ministry of Housing an Infrastructure Development,
Lusaka.

Dear Sir/Madam,

POWER OF ATTORNEY

**RE: TENDER FOR CONSTRUCTION OF A POST OFFICE TYPE 2 AND
ASSOCIATED EXTERNAL WORKS IN KANCHIBIYA DISTRICT- LB
No: MHID/PSU/W/04/2021**

WHEREAS Messrs Joseph Chirwa & Company who are established and reputable Legal
Practitioners and Notaries having registered offices at Plot 1, Manda Hill Road, Olympia
Park, Lusaka do confirm that we act for Awiki General Dealers Limited whose registered
office is Plot No.2, Off Japan Way, Woodlands, Lusaka and that the following person:

Mr. Joseph Chirwa (National Registration Card No.000000/11/1) is the Managing Director
of the company whose specimen signature appears below ....

Joseph Chirwa

In the presence of Company Secretary

For and on behalf of the Board of Directors

Is duly authorized to fully represent and sign all documentation relating to the above-named
Tender   and

subsequent contract on behalf of the Company.

Yours Faithfully,

Joseph and Company

Nyasha Chirwa

27th February, 2021

The Head of Procurement,
Ministry of Housing an Infrastructure Development,
Lusaka.

Dear Sir/Madam,

LITIGATION STATUS

RE: TENDER FOR CONSTRUCTION OF A POST OFFICE TYPE 2 AND ASSOCIATED EXTERNAL WORKS IN KANCHIBIYA DISTRICT- LB No: MHID/PSU/W/04/2021

We are legal advisers for Awiki General Dealers Limited for the past 3 years now and wish to advise that there are no legal proceedings against our client that we are aware of and that to the best of our knowledge and belief, there is no action or possible litigation that may have a material effect on the operation of the company.

The company is duly incorporated and validly existing in good standing under the laws of the Republic of Zambia and has the capacity to perform the obligation under the tender.

We trust that we have been of assistance in the matter and please do not hesitate to get in touch on any matter
 requiring clarity.

Yours faithfully,

Joseph Chirwa & Company

Nyasha Chirwa

DATED THE .... DAY OF 2021

GURU GENERAL DEALERS LIMITED

TO

LINDIWE CHIRWA

POWER OF ATTORNEY to deal and transact with business relating to the construction of 1 by 2 Classroom Block and Construction of 1 by Double VIP Latrine Toilet at Pembele Community School in Chirundu Ward of Chirundu Constituency in Lusaka Province in the Republic of Zambia (CTC/CDF/ORD/04/19) on behalf of **AWIKI GENERAL DEALERS LIMITED.**

POWER OF ATTORNEY IN RESPECT OF THE CONSTRUCTION OF 1 BY 2 CLASSROOM BLOCK AND CONSTRUCTION OF 1 BY DOUBLE VIP LATRINE TOILET AT PEMBELE COMMUNITY SCHOOL IN CHIRUNDU WARD OF CHIRUNDU CONSTITUENCY IN LUSAKA PROVINCE IN THE REPUBLIC OF ZAMBIA (CTC/CDF/ORD/04/19)

THIS POWER OF ATTORNEY is made on ....day of...................Two Thousand and nineteen by **AWIKI GENERAL DEALERS LIMITED**, a company duly registered in Zambia under Certificate No. 00000, whose

registered office is at Twin Tower Building, Room 5, 12th Floor, P.O. Box 1, Town Centre in the City and Province of Lusaka in the Republic of Zambia.

APPOINTMENT

Pursuant to resolutions of the 1st day of May Two Thousand and twenty-one, hereby appoint **LINDIWE CHIRWA**, holder of National Registration Card No. 000000/1/1 of Plot No. 1, Hollywood, Chirundu District in the City and Province of Lusaka in the Republic of Zambia, as the Company's Attorney; to do **ALL** things and execute **ALL** documents for the company, in relation to contract CTC/CDF/ORD/04/19 between the company and Chirundu Town Council.

IN RESPECT OF DOCUMENTS AND TITLE

The Attorney may receive and pursue all documents and money relating to the said contract until and upon its completion.

EXTENT OF POWERS

Generally, the Attorney may act in relation to the transactions relating to the completion of all activities leading to the completion of the said contract and may receive any money and incentives on behalf of the company in relation to the same contract.

The parts into which this Power of Attorney is divided are **NOT** exclusive of each other and any power given by it for any of its purposes may be used for any other purposes and independently of any other power.

EXECUTE DOCUMENTS

The Attorney may perform and carry into effect any agreement made with any other person in connection with transactions and complete such transactions by the execution of all necessary documents and the doing of any necessary act including the registration of any matter in any registry.

LEGAL PROCEEDINGS

The Attorney may bring, defend, settle or refer to arbitration any proceedings in connection with or incidental to the contract or monies and seek such remedies including damages or specific performance as he or she thinks fit.

IN WITNESS WHEREOF the parties hereto or their agents have hereunto set their seals and hands the day and year first before written.

THE COMMON SEAL of the said   )

was hereunto affixed.

in the presence of:

WITNESS

Name:.....................................

Address:....................................

Occupation:..............................

SIGNED by the said   )

LINDIWE CHIRWA) ....

in the presence of:

WITNESS

Name:......................................

Address:.......................................

Occupation:......................................

Duties of an attorney (or donee)

An attorney (or donor) is more or less a trustee holding a fiduciary position in trust on behalf of another. The duties of an attorney are similar to those of trustees and include the following:

(i) To act in accordance with the terms of that attorney's authority.

(ii) To act on behalf of and in the name of the donor (or principal).

(iii) To not exceed that attorney's authority.

(iv) To act with due care and reasonable skill.

(v) To not delegate that attorney's authority unless authorized to do so.

(vi) To avoid conflict of interest with that of the donor (or principal).

(vii) To not take advantage of that attorney's position to obtain a benefit for oneself.

(viii) To not accept a bribe.

(ix) To not make a secret profit.

(x) To account to the donor.

8.5 Termination of agency relationship

The agency relationship is a contractual and consensual relationship hence must come to an end. It is a relationship in which two parties mutually agree to enter and no party may be compelled or forced to be in such a relationship. In this regard, like all contractual relationships, the agency relationship may come to an end in any one of the following situations:

- By mutual agreement of the agent and principal
- By notice of either agent or principal on the other
- By unilateral withdrawal by either the agent or principal
- By expiration or effusion or lapse of time

- By operation of the law e.g. when the performance of the agency becomes illegal or impossible to perform

- By completion of the assignment

- By destruction of the subject matter of the agency relationship

- By dissolution of a corporation if either the agent or principal is a corporation

- By insanity, death or bankruptcy of the principal or agent

CHAPTER
9

CRIMINAL AND TORTIOUS LIABILITY

9.0 Introduction

This Chapter traverses the various aspects of criminal and tort law which professionals in the construction sector must be conversant with. It must be stated that the discussion is not conclusive but a mere introductory approach to the robust fields of criminal law and that of law of tort. The former deals with commission of crime which traditionally attracts penal sanctions while the latter deals with civil law and those found wanting are usually condemned to damages.

9.1 Criminal liability

What is criminal law?

Criminal law is the body of law dealing with the definition of what kinds of conduct, in what circumstances and with what concomitant mental or other factors, amount to crimes.[304] Criminal liability is therefore liability to be made subject to penalty, punishment, or treatment for having contravened a provision of the criminal law, as distinct from civil liability arising from breach of contract or commission of a tort among others.[305]

Definition of crime

There is no universally accepted definition of crime. Most definitions used depend on the orientation of a person who is trying to define the concept. Thus, sociologists will have a different definition from criminologists and *vice versa*. These and many examples show the diverse nature of scholars who have attempted to define this concept.

A crime is an act or omission which, whether or not it is morally wrongful or is deemed a wrong to an individual or civilly actionable by him or her for compensation for the harm done to him or her, is legally deemed an offence against the state or the community or the public and is punishable, as a deterrent to the offender and others, for the sake of public order, peace and well-being and in the interest of society.[306] In the case of *Board of Trade v Owen*[307] the word 'crime' was defined by the House of Lords to mean *"an unlawful act or default which is an offence against the public and renders the person guilty of the act liable to legal punishment"*. This definition though inconclusive by the

---

[304] The Oxford Companion to Law at p.316
[305] Ibid at p. 317
[306] Ibid at p. 313
[307] (1957) AC 602

account of many scholars brings out the following pertinent issues:

(i) It is an unlawful act or default;

(ii) It is an offence against the public;

(iii) That a person who commits it will be adjudged by a competent court as 'guilty' and as a criminal against the community as a whole;

(iv) That the convicted person will suffer some sort of penalty; and

(v) That the penalty imposed is a 'legal punishment', that is, punishment clearly specified in a statute or an Act of Parliament.[308]

Elements of crime[309]

The commission of crime generally requires, firstly, that the accused person committed an overt act of a kind deemed unlawful and criminal or allowed to happen what he or she could and should have prevented, or omitted to do something which by law he or she should have done and the failure to do what is deemed unlawful and criminal. This is what is called the *actus reus* element of crime. The act or omission must be voluntary, and in general there is no criminal liability for conduct which is involuntary by reason

---

[308] Kulusika, S.E. (2006). Text, Cases and Materials on Criminal Law in Zambia. Lusaka: University of Zambia Press at p.3
[309] The Oxford Companion to Law at p.314

of sleep, physical or mental defect or illness, or physical coercion.

The commission of crime generally requires, secondly, that the act or omission was done with a legally blameable condition of mind, usually called the *mens rea*. In common law crimes, the *mens rea* required varies: it may be a specific intention or either a specific intention or utter recklessness as to the consequences of conduct, or sometimes, serious negligence or disregard of foreseeable consequences. In statutory crimes, the requisite mental element may be defined by the statute, or the statute may be silent, in which case the court may infer that common law *mens rea* is required, or that liability exists for the wrongdoing, irrespective of *mens rea* what is called strict liability offences.

Accordingly, where a particular intent or state of mind is requisite for the crime, the accused may excuse himself or herself by disproving that he had the requisite state of mind, but did the act justifiably, or accidentally, or in ignorance, or had an honest belief in the existence of facts which, if they had existed, would have made this act innocent.

Relationship between mens rea and actus reus

A general rule of criminal law is that the *mens rea* (guilty mind) must exist in relation to the *actus reus* (guilty act). Thus, in other words, it is usually stated that there must be 'coincidence' of the *actus reus* and the *mens rea*.[310] It can be seen in the case of *Fagan v Metropolitan Police Commissioner*[311] that the defendant is capable of forming *mens rea* at a later stage in a sequence of events even if an initial act was not accompanied by *mens rea*.

Strict liability

Strict liability offences are offences for which no culpability needs to be established as liability is strict in that the prosecution need not prove the existence of *mens rea* in relation to one or more of the elements of the *actus reus*. This is opposed to many offences where a finding of culpability of blameworthiness is necessary for the imposition of criminal liability. The case of *Garmon Ltd v Attorney-General of Hong Kong*[312]lays out criteria, which is applied regularly as the appropriate test to determine whether an offence is one of strict liability as follows:

i. Type of offence

Strict liability is more likely to be imposed in relation to offences that:

a. Pertain to matters of social regulation and public welfare such as health, safety or road traffic.[313]

---

[310] See Thabo Meli v R [1954] 1 All ER 373 (Privy Council); and R v Shorty (1950) S.R. 280
[311] [1961] 1 QBD 439
[312] [1985] 1 AC 1 (Privy Council)
[313] See Patel's Bazaar Ltd v The People (1965) ZR 84 (CA)

a. Are regarded generally as only quasi-criminal that is little or no stigma attached to their commission.

b. Carry a light punishment, typically a fine.

ii. Statutory context

It has been repeatedly stated that the presumption of mens rea can only be displaced if this is clearly or by necessary implication the effect of statute. As the wording of the statute usually leaves the matter open, what is important is the statutory context of the provision in question.[314]

9.1.1 Corporate criminal liability

A corporate crime is any criminal offence committed by and hence chargeable to a corporate body (or body corporate) because of activities of its officers or employees such as tax evasion, under-declaration of profits, price fixing and toxic waste dumping among others. As stated earlier, a body corporate is deemed to be an artificial person at law and hence has a separate legal personality from its shareholders. In order for a body corporate to discharge its business it does so through the fora of its agents that is directors and employees. Therefore, subject to the concept of piercing the corporate veil, that body

---

[314] See Pharmaceutical Society of Great Britain v Storkwain Ltd (1986) 83 Cr. App. R. 359 (HL)

corporate must answer for its crimes or those committed in its name and on its behalf.[315]

Nature of corporate liability

The individualistic thesis of criminal responsibility which presupposes that individuals are autonomous hence free to control their decisions, including the choice to do wrong, does not naturally encompass artificial organisations such as companies. In this regard, it is often submitted that companies may only be criminally liable in two ways namely, vicarious liability and direct liability.

Firstly, under vicarious liability as with many offences of strict liability and negligence, a company can be liable vicariously for the acts of its directors, employees and agents in the course of their duties.[316] Whether vicarious liability applies or not is a matter of statutory interpretation, taking into account the policy of the law and whether vicarious liability will assist in the enforcement of that law.[317] Secondly, under direct liability which is also called as the identification doctrine, arises in situations where a company becomes liable to another for its own acts or omissions. The company is liable if in the course of its

[315] See Development Bank of Zambia v JCN Holdings Ltd and Others (Appeal No. 54/2016); Nampack Zambia Ltd v Copperfields Brewing Company Ltd, 2010/HN/149
[316] National Rivers Authority v Alfred McAlpine Homes East Ltd [1994] 4 All ER 286 (QBDC); see also Yusuf Vally and Another v Attorney-General, Appeal No. 50/2017 on the general principles of various liability of an employer for the wrongs of that employer's employees
[317] R v Gateway Foodmarkets Ltd [1997] 2 Cr. App. R. 40

business it causes harm or injury and must therefore, pay for the damage done and injury suffered. Officers and directors manage the enterprise, but do not by virtue of their positions have a claim to any residual gain from the enterprise.[318] In the case of *Tesco Supermarkets Ltd v Mattrass*[319] the local manager was not to be identified with the company, and therefore, he was another person and individually liable. In another case of *Meridian Global Funds Management Asia v Securities Commission*[320] the company was held liable as the investment officer was the controlling will and mind of the company.

9.2 Tortious liability[321]

The word *"tort"* comes from the Latin *tortus* which loosely means twisted or wrong. A tort is a civil wrong, as opposed to a crime, for which the remedy is a common law action for unliquidated (or unspecified or unquantified) damages and which is not exclusively the breach of a contract or the breach of trust or other equitable obligation.[322] It may be

---

[318] Robert B. Thompson, 'Unpacking Limited Liability: Direct and Vicarious Liability of Corporate participants for torts of the enterprise,' VLR Vol.47, Iss. 1 (1994)

[319] [1972] AC 153 (HL)

[320] [1995] 2 AC 500 (Privy Council)

[321] Excerpts from Chapter 1 in Chirwa, J. (2020). Chirwa on Tort: A Student Companion. Lusaka

[322] Heuston, R.V.F. and Buckley, R.A. (1996). Salmond and Heuston on the Law of Torts. London: Sweet and Maxwell at pp. 14-15

described as a wrong independent of contract, for which the appropriate remedy is a common law action.[323]

In simple terms, a tort is a civil wrong which is independent of implied contract for which the appropriate remedy is an action for unliquidated damages. What this means is that the wrong so causing injury must not arise either out of contract or criminal law. This is so because if it arises from contract then it is a matter enforceable under the terms of the contract. Similarly, if it arises out of breach of the criminal code, then it becomes a public issue prosecutable by the state.[324]

The law of tort is premised on the idea that hurt no one in words or actions couched as *"alterum non laedere"*. Thus, the law of torts serves the following functions and purposes:

- Provides remedies for wrongs;
- Provides compensation for loss;
- Acts as both individual and public deterrent;
- Provides protection to individuals and communities; and
- Acts as means for both corrective and distributive justice.

---

[323] M.A. Jones et al (eds.). (2017). Clerk and Lindsell on Torts. London: Sweet and Maxwell at p.1

[324] See Kumar, A. (2011). Law of Torts. New Delhi: Universal Law Publishing Co at pp.1-7

There are numerous subjects that one may encounter under the law of tort or torts. These include defamation, product liability, animal liability, trespass (to goods, land and person), and death in relation to tort and malicious falsehoods as well as prosecution among others. These may not be very compatible with the main theme of this book. However, we shall restrict our study to negligence, nuisance and trespass to land.

9.2.1 Negligence[325]

Negligence is the breach of a duty to take care that is imposed by either common law or statute law.[326] The ideas of negligence and duty of care are strictly correlative, and there is no such thing as negligence in the abstract; negligence is simply neglect of some care which we are bound by law to exercise towards somebody.[327] In short, negligence is the failure to use the requisite amount of care required by the law in the case where a duty to use care exists.[328] As a tort, negligence is a breach of a legal duty to take care which results in damage to the claimant.[329] It is an omission to do something which a reasonable man, guided upon those considerations which ordinarily regulate the

---

[325] Chapter 4 in Chirwa on Tort: A Student Companion
[326] Percy, R.A. and Walton, C.T. (1997). Charlesworth and Percy on Negligence. London: Sweet and Maxwell at p.3
[327] Thomas v Quatermaine (1887) 18 QB 685 at 694 per Bowen, LJ
[328] per Lord Porter in Riddell v Reid [1943] AC 1 at p. 31
[329] Rogers, W.V.H. (2010) at p.150

conduct of human affairs, would do, or doing something which a prudent and reasonable man would not do.[330]

Thus, to succeed under the tort of negligence, the defendant must prove the following elements which are discussed in detail below:

- That the defendant was under a *duty of care* to the plaintiff;

- That the defendant was in *breach of that duty*; and

- That as a result, the plaintiff has suffered *damage*.

9.2.2 Occupier's Liability[331]

Occupiers of premises owe a duty to take such care as in all the circumstances of the case is reasonable to see that visitors will be reasonably safe in using their premises for the purpose for which they are invited or permitted by the occupier to be there.[332] A person who has a sufficient degree of control over premises has a duty of care towards those who come lawfully on the premises.[333] Simply put, an occupier is the person in control of the property and ownership is irrelevant unless the owner is also in occupation. For one to be an occupier they must have immediate control and supervision of who comes on to the property. Therefore, control is a decisive factor and it is

---

[330] per Alderson, B in Blyth v Birmingham Waterworks Co. (1856) 11 Ex 751 at p.784

[331] Chapter 12 in Chirwa on Tort: A Student Companion

[332] The Oxford Companion to Law at p. 899

[333] Wheat v E. Lacon & Co Ltd [1966] AC 552

immaterial that the occupier has no interest in the property.[334]

The law on occupier's liability in Zambia is found under provisions of the *Occupier's Liability Act, Chapter 70 of the Laws of Zambia*. This is an Act to amend the law as to the liability of occupiers and others for injury or damage resulting to persons or goods lawfully on any land or other property from dangers due to the state of the property or to things done or omitted to be done there; and to provide for matters incidental to or connected therewith.[335] This statute has largely codified the common law position into legislation aimed at bridging the gap between the two.[336]

Section 3 (1) of the Occupiers' Liability Act provides that an occupier of premises owes the same duty, the *"common duty of care"*, to all his visitors, except in so far as he is free to and does extend, restrict, modify or exclude his duty to any visitor or visitors by agreement or otherwise. Thus, invitees and licensees at common law are all regarded as visitors and these visitors may be invited either expressly or impliedly. By sections 3 and 4 of the Occupier's Liability Act, the following persons are regarded as visitors:

    (i)   Persons entering under a contract;

---

[334] AMF International Ltd v Magnet Bowling Ltd [1968] 2 All ER 789
[335] Preamble to the Act
[336] Section 3 (2) of the Act

(ii)   Persons entering for the purpose of the occupier's business or for a business where both mutually benefit (invitee); and

(iii) Persons entering the premises with the permission of the occupier (licensee).

9.2.3   Strict liability[337]

Strict liability is liability without fault.[338] It is tortious liability imposed upon the defendant without the need for the plaintiff to prove intent, fault or negligence on the defendant's part. Liability is established provided that the plaintiff proves that it was the defendant's thing that caused them damage. It usually is liability imposed on the defendant for bringing unto their land dangerous things. Dangerous things are those things which are dangerous in themselves, irrespective of the use to which they are put or the circumstances of their use. Whether or not a thing is dangerous is a question of law.[339] The following things have been held to be *dangerous things* by courts:[340]

- Water artificially accumulated

- Sewage

- Fire

- Gas

---

[337] Chapter 10 in Chirwa on Tort: A Student Companion

[338] Goodwin v Reilley, 1 Dist., 176 Cal. App. 3d 86, 221, Cal.Rptr. 374,376

[339] Blacker v Lake and Elliot Ltd (1912) 106 LT 533; Read v J. Lyons and Co Ltd [1947] AC 156

[340] see Percy, R.A. and Walton, C.T. (1997) at pp. 887-892

- Electricity
- Poison
- Explosives
- Chemicals
- Acid
- Phosphorus
- Oil
- Paraffin

9.2.4 Nuisance[341]

Nuisance occurs when the defendant uses their land unreasonably to the detriment of his neighbour.[342] It is the *unlawful interference* with a person's use or enjoyment of land, or some other right over or in connection with. Thus, a plaintiff must show that they had some *proprietary rights* over land either as owner, leaseholder or tenant.[343] Other than this, the plaintiff must show that there was *unreasonable interference* with their land by the defendant. Unreasonable interference is established when the use of land by the defendant is such that it is in a way which would foreseeably interfere with the plaintiff's *quiet enjoyment* of their own land. It must be noted that some forms of public and statutory nuisances are crimes as well and thus one may

---

[341] Chapter 8 in Chirwa on Tort: A Student Companion
[342] per Denning, MR in Miller v Jackson [1977] QB 966 at p. 980
[343] see Malone v Laskey [1907] 2 KN 141; and Hunter v Canary Wharf [1997] AC 655

be liable to criminal prosecution. It is private nuisance that is traditionally a tort than a crime.

This tort primarily serves two purposes namely: it involves the protection of the use of land (or property) and secondly, that protection is from unreasonable interference. It is a branch of the law of tort most closely concerned with environmental protection in the modern day use of the word and actions under this tort have concerned:

- Water pollution
- Land pollution
- Air pollution
- Annoyance
- Pain
- Irritation

9.2.5   Trespass to land[344]

Trespass to land is committed by either entering upon the land in possession of the plaintiff unlawfully or remaining upon such land when asked to vacate the land, or by merely placing any object upon that land – in any of these cases without lawful justification- among others. It is actionable *per se* as it does require the defendant to prove actual damage.[345] Possession, which may be actual or constructive, means that the plaintiff continues to exercise a claim over

---

[344] Chapter 6 in Chirwa on Tort: A Student Companion
[345] Entick v Carrington (1765) 2 Wils. KB 275

the land to the exclusion of others in that land's use. Trespass to land involves interference with possession and hence ownership may not be relevant unless the owner is also in possession of the land, either actual or constructively.[346]

The other crucial element to be proved is that of entry. Entry must be present and must be shown to have occurred. It has to be noted that any intrusion on the land in possession of another without their consent, whether voluntary or by mistake, amounts to trespass.[347] However, entry which is involuntary, as opposed to that by mistake, may not amount to trespass as in situations where one is thrown or pushed unto someone's land.[348] The following acts by the defendant may amount to trespass:

- Placing a ladder against one's premises[349]
- Driving a nail into another person's wall[350]
- Growing a creeper upon someone's land[351]
- Placing rubbish against the wall of another[352]
- Remaining after the determination of a licence[353]

---

[346] see Towers and Co Ltd v Gray [1961] 2 QB 351
[347] Basely v Clarkson (1681) 3 Lev 37
[348] Smith v Stone (1647) 82 ER 533
[349] Wetripp v. Beldock, (1938) 2 All ER 779
[350] Lawrence v Obee (1814) 3 Camp 514
[351] Simpson v Weber (1925) 41 TLR 302
[352] Gregory v Piper [1829] 9 B & C 591
[353] Hurst v Picture Theatres Ltd [1915] 1 KB 1

- Use of entry other than that for which authorized to enter

Trespass Ab Initio

Ab initio is a Latin term meaning *"from the beginning."* Thus, if a person enters land under the authority of the person in possession, as a licensee, but ends up abusing that authority by either committing a *misfeasance* or *non-feasance* they are deemed to be trespassers from the beginning. The law considers this person to be a trespasser from the beginning and their authority to enter that land revoked retrospectively.[354]

---

[354] The Six Carpenters Case [1572] Eng R 452

CHAPTER

10

ENVIRONMENTAL LAW AND POLICY

10.0   Introduction

This Chapter examines the aspects of environmental rules and regulations as they relate to the construction sector. The chapter builds up on previous chapters that have touched on the aspects of environmental regulation in one way or another. Environmental law is a nestling of common law areas such as tort chief of which touches on province of nuisance and trespass.

10.1   Definition of environment

The environment is the totality of physical, economic, cultural, aesthetic, and social circumstances and factors which surround and affect the desirability and value of property and which also affect the quality of peoples' lives.[355] It comprises the natural or man-made surroundings at any place, comprising air, water, land, natural resources, animals, buildings and other constructions.[356]Generally, the

---

[355] Black's Law Dictionary at p. 534

[356] Section 2 of the Environmental Management Act No. 12 of 2011 (hereinafter referred to as the "EMA")

environment comprises the space, land and soil, water and air and everything inside or on them.

10.2   Duty to protect environment

Every person has a duty to co-operate with State organs, State institutions and other persons to—

(a) maintain a clean, safe and healthy environment;

(b) ensure ecologically sustainable development and use of natural resources;

(c) respect, protect and safeguard the environment; and

(d) prevent or discontinue an act which is harmful to the environment.[357]

It is also law in Zambia that every person has a duty to safeguard and enhance the environment and to inform the Zambia Environmental Management Agency (ZEMA) and other appropriate authorities of any activity or phenomenon that affects or may affect the environment.[358] This is premised on the fact that every person living in Zambia has the right to a clean, safe and healthy environment.[359]

---

[357] Article 256 of Constitution
[358] Section 6 of EMA; see section 2 on a list of other appropriate authorities and their legislative framework
[359] Section 4 of EMA

10.3   Principles of environmental management

The principles of environmental management in Zambia emanate from the Constitution of Zambia. Part XIX of the Constitution provides for a roadmap on matters related to land, environment and natural resources. Article 255 of the Constitution outlines the underlying principles on the management and development of the country's environment and natural resources whose goal is to secure a clean, health and safe environment for the sustainable development of the country. In this line, the state is required, in the utilisation of natural resources and management of the environment to:

a. Protect genetic resources and biological diversity;

b. Implement mechanisms that minimise waste;

c. Promote appropriate environment management systems and tools;

d. Encourage public participation;

e. Protect and enhance the intellectual property in, and indigenous knowledge of, biodiversity and genetic resources of local communities;

f. Ensure that the environmental standards enforced in zambia are of essential benefit to citizens; and

g. Establish and implement mechanisms that address climate change.[360]

---

[360] Article 257 of Constitution

The EMA brings out two important principles regarding environmental management in Zambia. These principles are of paramount importance to players in the construction industry. The two principles under consideration are the *precautionary principle* and the *polluter pays principle.*[361] Precautionary principle means the principle that, lack of scientific certainty should not be used as a reason to postpone measures to prevent environmental degradation, or possible environmental degradation, where there is a threat of serious or irreversible environmental damage, because of the threat.[362] On the other hand, *"polluter pays principle"* means the principle that the person or institution responsible for pollution or any other damage to the environment shall bear the cost of restoration and clean-up of the affected area to its natural or acceptable state.[363]

10.4   Pollution control

The major environmental crime that players in the construction sector commit is pollution. This is not to downplay other crimes that are found in legislation that we have covered in the foregoing chapters regarding planning, survey, permits and the like. Pollution means the presence in the environment of one or more contaminants or pollutants in such quantities and under such conditions as may cause discomfort to, or endanger, the health, safety

[361] Section 6 of EMA lays out the principles governing environmental management
[362] Section 2
[363] id

and welfare of human beings, or which may cause injury or damage to plant or animal life or property, or which may interfere unreasonably with the normal enjoyment of life, the use of property or conduct of business.[364] The law prohibits discharges into the environment that may cause pollution to the environment. Section 32 of the EMA provides that:

(1) A person shall not, without a licence, discharge, cause or permit the discharge of a contaminant or pollutant into the environment if that discharge causes, or is likely to cause, an adverse effect.

(2) A person who operates a motor vehicle, boat, train, aircraft or other similar conveyance shall not—

   a. Operate the conveyance in a manner that is likely to cause the discharge of a contaminant or pollutant in contravention of the prescribed emission standards; or

   b. Import any machinery, equipment, device or similar thing likely to cause the emission of a contaminant or pollutant into the environment in contravention of prescribed emission standards.

(3) A person who contravenes this section commits an offence   and is liable, upon conviction, to a fine not exceeding seven hundred thousand penalty units

---

[364] id

or to imprisonment for a period not exceeding seven years, or to both.

(4) In addition to a sentence that the court may impose under subsection (3), the court may direct the person to—

    a. Clean up the polluted environment and remove the effects of pollution to the satisfaction of the Agency; and

    b. Pay the full cost of cleaning the polluted environment and of removing the pollution.

(5) Without prejudice to the provisions of subsections (3) and (4), the court may direct the polluter to meet the cost of the pollution to any third parties affected by the pollution caused by that person, through adequate compensation, restoration or restitution.

There is need for permission for any person to emit or discharge a pollutant[365] or contaminant[366] into the environment.[367] By Part IV of the EMA the following

---

[365] *"pollutant"* includes any substance whether liquid, solid or gaseous which— (a) may, directly or indirectly, alter the quality of any element of the receiving environment; or (b) is hazardous or potentially hazardous to human health or the environment; and includes objectionable odours, radio-activity, noise, temperature change or physical, chemical or biological change to any segment or element of the environment as per section 2

[366] *"contaminant"* means a substance, physical agent, energy or a combination of substances and physical agents, that may contribute to, or create a condition of, pollution as per section 2

[367] Section 33

---

aspects of pollution to the environment have been recognized and measures put in place to control them:

- Water pollution (Sections 45 t048)

- Air pollution (Sections 49 to 52)

- Waste management (Sections 53 to 63)

- Pesticides and toxic substances (Sections 64 to 66)

- Noise pollution (Sections 67 to 70)

- Ionization radiation (Sections 71 to 73)

- Natural resources management (Sections 74 to 83)

It is a duty of every person not only to protect the environment but also to report discharge into the environment[368] and to inform ZEMA and other appropriate agencies at the earliest planning stage on an intention to erect, install or develop a new industrial facility or plant, an agricultural scheme, business or any other undertaking that is likely to emit or discharge any pollutant or contaminant into the environment.[369]

10.5   Environmental offences

The EMA has in it provisions that have criminalized certain actions and conduct relating to the use of the environment. Parts XI and XII of the Act have made the following actions and conduct offences under the criminal law of

---

[368] Section 35
[369] Section 36

Zambia which may be committed by both natural and artificial persons:[370]

(i) Offences relating to environmental impact assessment (Section 118)

(ii) Offences relating to returns and records (Section 119)

(iii) Offences relating to environmental standards (Section 120)

(iv) Offences relating to biological diversity (Section 121)

(v) Offences relating to hazardous waste materials, chemicals and radio-active substances (Section 122)

(vi) Offences relating to pesticides and toxic substance (Section 123)

(vii) Offences relating to protected areas (Section 124)

(viii) General penalties relating to pollution or breach of any provision of the EMA (Section 125)

It is crucial to consider the fact that environmental law does not exist in isolation. In fact, as section 2 of the EMA

---

[370] Section 126 of EMA provides that *"Where an offence under this Act is committed by a body corporate or an unincorporate body, every director or manager of the body corporate or unincorporate body shall be liable, upon conviction, as if the director or manager had personally committed the offence, unless the director or manager proves to the satisfaction of the court that the act constituting the offence was done without the knowledge, consent or connivance of the director or manager or that the director or manager took reasonable steps to prevent the commission of the offence"*

shows, environmental law overlaps many other areas of law. In this regard, the EMA exists not in isolation but in tandem with a plethora of statutes most of which have been discussed in the foregoing chapters. Thus, the EMA must not be considered as a standalone Act but must be read together with many other statutes that aim at protecting the environment overall and regulating its use specifically. That said, the above list is not exhaustive of what are termed as environmental offences.

REFERENCES

American Law Institute (2006). Restatement of the Law of Agency, 3rd edn., Minnesota: Thomson Reuters

Atiyah, P.S. (1975). The Sale of Goods, 5th edn., London: Pitman

Birds, J. (2013). Birds' Modern Insurance Law, 9th edn., London: Sweet and Maxwell

Black, H.C. et al (1990). Black's Law Dictionary, 6th edn., Minnesota: West Publishing Co.

Cane, P. (2006). Atiyah's Accidents, Compensation and the Law. Cambridge: Cambridge University Press

Chirwa, J. (2019). The Right to Life and Occupational Health and Safety in Zambia. Beau Bassin: Lambert Academic Publishing

Chirwa, J. (2020). Chirwa on Tort: A Student Companion. Lusaka

Chirwa, J. (2020). Commentary on Public Law in Zambia: Law, Politics and Governance. Claremont: Juta and Company (Pty) Ltd

Chirwa, J. (2020). Essential Text on Local Government Law in Zambia. Claremont: Juta and Company (Pty) Ltd

Chungu, C. and Beele, E. (2018). Labour Law in Zambia: An

Introduction. Claremont: Juta and Company (Pty) Ltd

Chungu, C. and Beele, E. (2020). Labour Law in Zambia: An Introduction, 2nd edn. Claremont: Juta and Company (Pty) Ltd

Cranston, R. (1984). Consumer Protection and the Law, 2nd edn., London: Weidenfeld and Nicolson

CUTS, 'Enforcing Competition Law in Zambia', ZCA/CUTS (2002)

Dada, T.O. (2006). General Principles of Law, 3rd edn, Lagos: T.O. Dada and Co

Davies, P.L. (2003). Gower's Principles of Modern Company Law, 6th edn., London: Sweet & Maxwell

Gates, R. B. (2018). Gates on Understanding Company Law: A Conceptual and Functional Approach. Lusaka: Reagan Blankfein Gates

Goodman, A.H. (2004). Basic Skills for the New Arbitrator, 2nd edn., Rockville: Solomon Publications

Goodman, A.H. (2005). Basic Skills for the New Mediator, 2nd edn., Rockville: Solomon Publications

GRZ (2015). Report of the Auditor General on the Management of Occupational Safety and Health. Lusaka: OAG

Heuston, R.V.F. and Buckley, R.A. (1996). Salmond and Heuston on the Law of Torts. London: Sweet and Maxwell

Heyton, D. (1982). Megarry's Manual of the Law of Real Property, 6th edn., London: ELBS

Ivamy, E.R.H (1975). Underhill's Principles of the Law of Partnership, 10th edn., London: Butterworths

Joseph Chirwa, 'The Benefits of Alternative Dispute Resolution to a Country's Legal System and its extent of usage in Zambia: An Assessment,' LLB Thesis (Zambian Open University, 2014)

Kanja, G.M. (2006). Intellectual Property Law. Lusaka: UNZA Press

Kulusika, S.E. (2006). Text, Cases and Materials on Criminal Law in Zambia. Lusaka: University of Zambia Press

Kumar, A. (2011). Law of Torts. New Delhi: Universal Law Publishing Co

Lubumbe, J.K. (2017). Land Acquisition and Tiltling Procedures in Zambia. Ndola: Mission Press

M, Woodley (ed.). (2005). Osborn's Concise Law Dictionary. London: Sweet & Maxwell

M.A. Jones et al (eds.). (2017). Clerk and Lindsell on Torts. London: Sweet and Maxwell

Malila, M. (2006). Commercial Law in Zambia: Cases and Materials. Lusaka: UNZA Press

Malila, M. and Chungu, C. (2019). The Law of Business Associations in Zambia: An Introduction. Claremont: Juta and Company

Mudenda, F.S. (2007). Land Law in Zambia: Cases and Materials. Lusaka: UNZA Press

Mwenda, W.S. (2011). Employment Law in Zambia: Cases and Materials. Lusaka: UNZA Press

Nolan-Haley, J.M. (2008). Alternative Dispute Resolution. Minnesota: Thomson/West

Peel, E. (2011). Treitel's Law of Contract, 13th edn., London: Sweet and Maxwell

Percy, R.A. and Walton, C.T. (1997). Charlesworth and Percy on Negligence. London: Sweet and Maxwell

Pitt, G. (2004). Employment Law, 5th edn., London: Sweet & Maxwell

Reynolds, F. (2006). Bowstead and Reynolds on Agency, 18th edn., London: Sweet and Maxwell

Riddal, J.G. (1988). Introduction to Land Law, 4th edn., London: Butterworths

Robert B. Thompson, 'Unpacking Limited Liability: Direct and Vicarious Liability of Corporate participants for torts of the enterprise,' VLR Vol.47, Iss. 1 (1994)

Sealy, L.S. and Hooley, R.J.A. (2009). Commercial Law: Text, Cases, and Materials, 4th edn., Oxford: Oxford University Press

Singer, R.M. (1980). Contemporary Business Law: Principles and Cases. New York: McGraw-Hill Book Co.

Turpin, C. and Tomkins, A. (2007). British Government and the Constitution, 6th edn., Cambridge: Cambridge University Press

Walker, D.M. (1980). The Oxford Companion to Law. Oxford: Clarendon Press

Wayne Barnes, 'Arrested Development: Rethinking the Contract Age of Majority for the Twenty-first Century Adolescent,' 76 MD. L.REV. 405 (2017)

Winnie Sithole Mwenda, 'Paradigms of Alternative Dispute Resolution and Justice Delivery in Zambia,' LLD Thesis (UNISA, 2006)

www.ingramcontent.com/pod-product-compliance
Lightning Source LLC
Chambersburg PA
CBHW060007210326
41520CB00009B/853